HAIDA EAGLE TREASURES

HAIDA EAGLE TREASURES

Traditional Stories and Memories from a Teacher of the Tsath Lanas Clan

PANSEY COLLISON
with original artwork by
Paul White

18 19 20 21 6 5 4 3 2

Brush Education Inc.
www.brusheducation.ca
contact@brusheducation.ca

Cover design by Dean Pickup
Printed and manufactured in Canada

Library and Archives Canada Cataloguing in Publication

Collison, Pansy, author
Haida eagle treasures : traditional stories and memories from a teacher of the Tsath Lanas clan / Pansy Collison.
Previously published: Haida eagle treasures : Tsath Lanas history and narratives / Pansy Collison. Calgary : Detselig Enterprises, 2010.
Issued in print and electronic formats.
ISBN 978-1-55059-748-6 (softcover).--ISBN 978-1-55059-749-3 (PDF)
1. Collison, Pansy. 2. Haida women--Biography. 3. Haida Indians. I. Title.
E99.H2C657 2017 971.1'1200497280092 C2017-905998-X
C2017-905999-8

Funded by the Government of Canada
Financé par le gouvernement du Canada
Canada

I dedicate this book to my family: my mother, Gertie White; my husband, Art Collison; and my children. I also dedicate this book to our Hereditary Chief: Ken Edgars and the *Tsath Lanas* Eagle Clan from Naden Harbour, *Kung,* and North Island.

Contents

Acknowledgements

It is with great gratitude that I thank Isabelle (Hill) Lewis, Jo Scott, Isaac White, and Art Collison for proofreading my book. I thank my cousin Dr. Frederick White for the meticulous editing and proofreading as well as providing guidance in writing my book. Thank you to Jamie Scott for teaching me various tips and tricks to use the computer. Thank you to Dr. George Deagle for providing a review of my book. Thank you to Hereditary Chief *Thasi,* Mr. Ken Edgars, and my grandmother, the Late Amanda Edgars, for giving me permission to write the stories about our clan. Thank you to Douglas Williams and Lena Edgars for giving me permission to write the Golden Spruce story. I thank my mother, Gertie White, for all her support and guidance in validating the Haida stories and sharing her life history with me for everyone to read and enjoy.

Preface

The material here is one of a kind among all the books published on or about Haida culture. The most important factor is that the author is not simply someone who has spent time studying the Haida people and culture, though she has studied both. It is not only that she has spent time studying the Haida language with Elders, listening to the stories of old, recording them, and then presenting them here. Rather, the difference is that the culture and language she studied are her own. The Haida Elders she spoke with were not simply informants about linguistic or cultural information – they were her close relatives. In fact, no Elder gave the author more insight into the richness of Haida culture than her own mother.

Some of the great differences we see in other books about Haida culture and this book are related to the reasons for researching, documenting, transcribing, writing, and revising. Previous research on the Haida – its people, culture, language, and history – has been conducted because of various motivations. A master's thesis, a doctoral dissertation, or an item on list for tenure or promotion are academic explanations for such endeavors, though other times it may be love, respect, or even intrigue with Haida culture that sparks such responses. Historically, such research has benefited the Haida community little because, though the Haida have been the target of the research, they have not been the audiences for the research. It usually has been the mainstream or academic community that served as the audiences for the books and articles published. This book reverses that trend. While certainly including the mainstream audience because of the wealth of narrative and cultural content, it is for the Haida community first and foremost.

Moreover, the author's own purpose sets this book apart, for her intention is to honor the memory of her mother and grandmother. Honor, and its reciprocity, is deeply rooted in Haida culture and is one of the most important aspects of Haida interrelationships. The author has chosen to devote this book to what she has learned and gained from the most important relationship in the Haida community, her mother.

The book is full of oral history, contemporary issues in the Haida community and in First Nations communities, and personal narratives and poems of her place in that society. She documents her own participation in two cultures: her place within Haida traditions and her role as a teacher in mainstream culture.

That she is an *insider* sets her apart as a researcher and writer of Haida history and culture. She is not from some other part of the world and will not be going back there after she has published this book. She is from the area and will remain in the area long after the book is on the shelf. Being an insider affords greater familiarity with Haida culture, simply on the basis of ownership and identity. The narratives she writes about Haida culture and history are not separate from her own history; they are her history. But far from the mainstream notion that indigenous people cannot objectively study their own cultures, this book proves that being indigenous does not invalidate any attempt to be academic as well. While the negative notion that indigenous people are unqualified to study their own culture objectively remains largely unchallenged, this book by its existence challenges any such notion.

It is Pansy Collison's connection to Haida culture that unifies her personal narrative with her mother's or the other Elders she is involved with as she learns the language, stories, and skills that her mother and grandmothers have passed down to her. The bond to Haida history and identities are integral throughout the Elder's stories and in her personal narrative. As she prepares for life and then encounters life in the mainstream, the lessons from her Haida apprenticeship become a springboard for creativity and a foundation to endure and overcome hardships. She becomes a role model along the way and a mentor to those who aspire to do the same. All these efforts and experiences combine to infuse her contributions to the career she has chosen, being a teacher.

For First Nations and Native American students, the path to formal education is difficult. The obstacles just to graduate from high school are great. Of the few First Nations persons that succeed in higher education, even fewer return to their community after they have finished college. What usually happens is that the education gained has indeed equipped the student with marketable skills that employers desire, but these jobs are most often away from the home community – especially the reserve. Thankfully, this is not the case with the author. Her pursuit of formal education was focused on teaching close to her home. Her teaching skills, artistic talents, and political affiliations keep her involved in the education and political endeavors on Haida Gwaii, and her accounts of the journey reveal both the joys and hardships along the way.

Finally, there is a venture and challenge in going public with a book like this because the stories and events that the author deals with will certainly have different experiences among the readers, but this is no reason for being silenced. Her accounts of the stories are based on interviews and declarations of Haida Elders and she is merely summarizing the accounts and presenting them to us. It is an authentic voice of an insider that offers a glimpse of Haida culture that others have yet to capture or express.

Frederick White, Ph.D.

(back left to right) Geeda Jones, Helmer Smith, Adeline Penna, Calvin Bell, Rose Bell; (front left to right) Gertie White, Art Collison, Pansy Collison, Katie Collison

(left to right) Pansy Snow White, Darleen White, Kathleen White, Pansy Collison, Erica Collison

Ben White, Geraldine Angus

Kathleen White, John Paul White, Mary White, Paul White, Rodney White, Pansy Snow White

Paul and Mary White's wedding party

(back left to right) Erica Collison, Tatzen Collison, Pansy Collison, Art Collison, Stolly Collison; (front left to right) Gertie White, Kwiiaas Parnel

Art and Pansy Collison

(back left to right) John Paul White, Pansy Snow White, Rodney White; (middle left to right) Kathleen White, Darleen White; front, Sharleen White

Weaving by Pansy Collison

Book Review

Pansy Collison has written a deceptively simply yet marvelously complex series of stories that blend past with present in a way that accurately reflects both these influences on the life of the modern Haida.

As the family doctor in Old Massett for much of the modern period described, I was privileged to watch many of the events that Pansy describes, and I witnessed the lifecycle of many of her family members unfold. Her accounts accurately reflect the mysterious blend of traditional myths with pragmatic reality that forge modern Haida people, who are unlike any other culture on earth. The wondrous natural world of Haida Gwaii continues to be a crucible where stories perpetuate values required to survive in the dynamic, changing world.

Dr. George Deagle

About the Author

Pansy Collison is a Haida woman born and raised at Old Massett, B.C. Haida Gwaii. She has extensive dynamic knowledge of the Haida traditions and culture, and she shares this knowledge as a teacher, singer, and storyteller. She is also a creative artist who makes drums, traditional button blankets, vests, regalia, weaving cedar hats, vases, and baskets. Amidst these other talents she also coordinates and organizes the Haida Eagle Dance group. It is her goal and obligation to teach the songs to the younger *Tsath Lanas* generation and maintain continuity in the Haida culture to keep the Haida culture thriving, alive, and flourishing.

Pansy has an extensive education. She graduated and received her high school diploma from Prince Rupert Senior Secondary School. In 1970 she obtained a Small Business Management Certificate from Camosun College in Victoria, B.C. She continued her education to obtain an Early Childhood Certificate. In 1976 to 1978 she went to the University of British Columbia attending the First Nations Education Degree program and returned to Massett to get married in 1979. She worked in various positions for the Massett Band Council and she taught Nursery students for three years at Chief Matthews School. She proceeded to work as a bookkeeper for the Haida Cedar Products. During this period in her life, she utilized her business education to operate her own gift shop, Haida Islands Gift Shop. While she owned and operated her business; she also worked as a Relief clerk for the Canadian Armed Forces Station, Invigilator for North West Community College, Census worker, and confidential secretary for Dr. Schofield.

In 1992, she moved to Prince Rupert with her family to further her education. After she obtained her first degree in General Studies and Teacher's Certificate, she worked as an

Instructor for North West Community College, teaching the art of button blanket making. She was also a First Nations Instructor for the Futures, Quest and Adult programs at Friendship House. From 1995 to 2006 she worked for the Role Model Program for School District #52, teaching the First Nations culture and traditions in all grade levels.

Pansy's education is extensive and includes a Small Business Management Certificate, Early Childhood Certificate, Post Baccalaureate Diploma (SFU), Adult Instructor Diploma (Vancouver College), Teacher's Certificate, Bachelors of General Studies, and Masters in Curriculum and Instruction (SFU). During her teaching career she also completed two courses in the Masters degree in Counseling (UBC). She also has to her credit education in basic accounting and bookkeeping, Pittman shorthand, Income tax workshops, Conflict Resolution workshops, Stress Management, Financial and Entrepreneur workshops, and Business Development.

Pansy is the spokesperson for Chief *Thasi,* Ken Edgars. She provides advice and direction, and she assists the *Tsath Lanas* clan in political, economic, and social endeavors. She is proactive in protecting their land and extremely vocal in voicing concerns in the political arena. She spent twelve years as a Council member and four years as Deputy Chief Councilor for Old Massett Band.

Her published writings include a story called "The Greatest Mentor in My Life" in *The En'owkin Journal of First North American Peoples* (1996), edited by Damm-Akiwenzie and Armstrong. She is one of the First Nations teachers who contributed to writing their stories about the struggles and dilemmas in the teaching profession in the mainstream education. These vignettes were collected in a book called *First Nations Teachers; Identity and Community, Struggles and Change* (2008), edited by June Beynon. Pansy has been teaching for eighteen years: three years in Old Masset, B.C. and fifteen years in Prince Rupert, B.C. She continues to teach and she enjoys teaching primary grade levels in Prince Rupert. She also teaches adult workshops in the art of drums, weaving, and traditional regalia. She has lived in an elegant generation of time where she was taught by many cultural professors of the Haida culture. Now she is sharing her wealth of knowledge with others to learn and appreciate the Haida culture, through her voice as an insider.

About the Illustrator

Paul White Jr. is a Haida carver who has carved all his life. He has an incredible gift to carve rings, pendants, and earrings in silver and gold. He carves head pieces for traditional dancers and he has carved several totem poles over sixty feet tall. He carved a memorial totem pole for his grandmother, the Late Amanda Edgars. Initially, he learned how to carve by observation. Paul has expanded his artistic abilities in designing over a hundred Haida designs on silkscreen prints. He designs clothing, and regalia, and his amazing designs adorn vests, blazers, and button blankets. He is an illustrator for the book *Haida Art,* which is one of the series for the *Queen Charlotte Island Readers.*

Paul is blessed with seven children: Rodney, John Paul, Pansy Snow White, twins Kathleen and Darleen, Sharleen, and his late daughter Colleen. He has three grandchildren and has been married to his loving wife, Mary Ethel for twenty-eight years.

Although Paul was unfortunately struck with Parkinson's disease, he has a strong-willed spirit and he continues to paint designs, carve silver, gold pendants, and carve headpieces from cedar wood. He is teaching his son John Paul and his nephew Fraser Williams how to carve out of silver and gold. He also teaches anyone who is willing to learn how to carve out of silver and gold. My brother, Paul enjoys teaching anyone who is willing to learn how to make silkscreen prints and print designs on t-shirts. He prints designs on t-shirts and silk screens for various potlatch's and headstone moving events to be given away as gifts.

Paul is a remarkable role model for his children and the people of Haida Gwaii. He has a quiet demeanor and he displays his kindness by loving all his children and grandchildren. Paul is a fine example of one of the great Haida artists in this modern day.

Introduction:

Celebrating Haida Culture through Storytelling

The greatest gift a person can have is to know their identity and their culture. Who are you? Where do you come from? When you know your own history, culture, stories, crests, names, and songs, you are proud of who you are. When you know who you are, you have respect for yourself. You will have a positive attitude towards life and towards other people. You will have empowerment and ambition to pursue your goals. These accomplishments build your self-esteem. I am a Haida woman. I know who I am. I know where I come from. I am proud of my culture and heritage.

Born and raised in the beautiful mystical Islands of Haida Gwaii, this is my home where my family and I grew up. This is where my husband and I go to dig razor clams, and where my children and I go to swoop for crabs with our nets on the exquisite sandy beaches at *Tow* Hill. This is where my sister Adeline Penna and I go beach combing along the shores collecting gorgeous colorful agates, picking abalone and clams after a big North windstorm. I remember the exciting and challenging times when my sister Rose Bell and I travelled up to the Yakoun River to set up our nets across the river to catch our own sockeye, and this is where Rose and I courageously went out hunting for deer along the roads at Juskatla. I was taught all my life to listen and learn from our Elders. We were brought up in a gentle, but disciplined manner and we were taught at a young age how to work, maintain our integrity, and learn our culture. Children were encouraged to assume responsibility early in life and to work with and learn from adults. In a society in which individual experience was particularly valued, elders were expected to pass their knowledge on to younger people, both orally and by demonstration (Cruikshank, 1995, p. 10). These Islands are our ancient home where our great powerful ancestors have lived since time immemorial. The Haida have lived on Haida Gwaii (formerly known as Queen Charlotte Islands) for the last nine millennia, according to the curator of Canada's National Museum (Johnson, 1987). Our Elders always tell us that we have lived here from the beginning of time. This book is a personal account of Haida history and culture that blends my personal voice with the Elder's voices, especially my mother's and grandmother's.

My book is the first of its kind to be told and written by a Haida woman. Frederick White, Ph.D., a tall, good-looking, intelligent Haida, also wrote a book called *Ancestral Language Acquisition among Native Americans: A study of a Haida Language Class*, published in 2008. Dr. White teaches composition, linguistics, and literature in the English department at Slippery Rock University, Pennsylvania. His research interests are vast, but he also has a major focus on linguistic and literacy fields, including Native American and First Nations cultural issues such as history, identity, Haida language revitalization, oral literature, education, and contact narratives. Dr. White is from the *Tsath Lanas* Eagle Clan. His mother's name is Margaret Bernhard. His grandfather's name is Clement White. Clement and my dad, Paul White, are brothers. Dr. White travels all over Canada and United States sharing his knowledge in education and First Nations culture to professional teachers at workshops and as a keynote speaker in education conferences. As teachers, Frederick and I are role models for the First Nations children and Haida communities. Teachers bring with them not only their fund of knowledge but also their culturally patterned ways of organizing and passing on that knowledge. Even more fundamentally, they bring the value systems of their communities concerning what is important to learn and how most appropriately to learn. Native traditions teachers are considered an integral part of the knowledge they possess, and their ways of teaching are as important as the knowledge itself. (Cooley & Ballenger, 1982)

I spent eight years in university and I have read many books on First Nations people. Many books have been written by anthropologists or researchers or linguistics that come to First Nations communities to research, study, and write life histories of First Nations people. Over the last century several authors have written about the Haida people (listed chronologically, Swanton, 1905a, 1905b, 1911, 1912; Curtis, 1970; Blackman, 1982; Drew, 1982; Cogo & Cogo, 1983; Enrico, 1986; Boelscher, 1989; Henley, 1989; MacDonald, 1994; Enrico, 1994, 1995; Enrico & Stuart, 1996; Turner, 2004; White, 2008). My efforts and goals in writing this book are to reach not only the audiences of non-native people, teachers, and children, but also to inspire the Haida community especially, where this book will perhaps encourage other clans from the Raven and Eagle moieties to write their history.

In their book *In Celebration of Our Survival,* Jensen and Brooks (1991) send an invitation out to aboriginal people to create a self-portrait of First Nations people: For years and years we as aboriginal people have been studied, observed and written about, generally by non-aboriginal writers (p. 9). They further state, "and sometimes even as fascinating anthropological specimens" (p. 9). While all of us who have been in the feast halls and have been involved in Indian organizations have heard the correct versions of our history and our leaders' plans and visions for the future, many people have not had the opportunity to be there and to hear this information first hand without the biases and slants of observers and interpreters. They further state: A portrait that will tell people who we really are, what we are doing, and our plans, hopes and dreams. We want to portray our strengths, accomplishments, contributions and visions. (p. 9) This is one of the purposes of my book, to portray our identity, pride, traditions, and culture, and tell people I am proud of our Haida heritage and culture.

My purpose is to emphasis that every culture, clan, and community has their own set of values, traditions, and beliefs. My husband, Art Collison, captures some of the concepts of our culture, spirituality, compassion, and family in the poem he wrote as follows:

Haida Gwaii Spirit (September 4, 1991)

My heart is the sea, like a caring father, with the inherent wisdom our forefathers had for thousands of years.
My breath is the four winds, like a loving mother, breathing the breath of life into us since the dawning of the four seasons of time.
My blanket is the warm comforting thoughts of our loved ones silently drifting over the cool blue sea, like grandmother passes her heartfelt love unto her children's children forever from land to sea, for she is our guiding light to life.
My feet are the earth, like a noble grandfather welcoming us home from a windswept sea.
The spirited wake of seafaring, cedar-crafted canoes surging upon the seashore, paddles dipping into ice waters in perfect harmony with beating drums and vibrant voices singing victorious sea songs.
Happy families descending upon the pebbly beaches as Haida sea hunters return from a call to venture over the enchanting deep blue sea.
Exciting distant images of the past lingering in the outer reaches of my mind, caught up in the wonderment of the vast changing times.
My spirit is nature dancing with the spirits of every living creature created by our ancestors who carved our totem poles which stand in the villages of our mystical Island called Haida Gwaii.
As our Elders live and love, remember to follow in their

wise footsteps unto a pathway of peace and prosperity to a happy, fulfilling future life.

Cherish and share the loving memories of your parents and Elders. Let the happiness of their cheerful spirits shine around you like a bright and sunny day. They'll be there with a warm, loving heart.

Our children play harmoniously in the sunshine, gleefully calling one another's names with joyous laughter, their sounds drifting along in the gentle summer breeze. Little feet dancing in rhythm with the glittering ripple of the sea.

Listening to the melodious sounds of children playing with blessings from the heavenly skies leaves me content as the evening draws near.

As the sun sets over the western sea our evening sky is a peaceful glow. We're grateful for the riches from our ocean, mountains, valleys, trees, lakes, rivers. Always care deeply for Mother Nature.

As stars have eternally shone into the universe so will the spirits of the Haida Nation shine with pride and honor forever.

As the starlit sky dances with the brilliance of the northern lights may our spirits unite with our brothers and sisters of the First Nations for us to live in oneness.

Let the pride of our wise heritage inspire us to live in harmony with the spirits of our exalted First Nations.

In the chain of life, should a link become tarnished or broken, forge the link together with love, peace, honesty and forgiving kindness. Through your strength and courage inspire each new generation to forgiveness for it is the beginning of a peaceable, intellectual, existence.

Like the keen eyes and powerful wings of the soaring eagles, the spirits of our ancestors eternally watch over this vast ancient land and sea.

(A. Collison, 1993, p. 43)

When First Nations people learn their history, language, and culture, they will gain a sense of pride in their heritage and a sense of validity of their culture. Many First Nations children did not have the opportunity to learn their languages. My sister, Rose Bell remembers when she went to Residential School. She states the following:

> The government wanted to turn us into white people. Our cultural family units were broken apart. Also, part of becoming 'white' was to speak English. Because my parents also attended residential school, they didn't see the value in teaching us our language. The Indian Agent told them not to speak to their children in Haida because it would not help them in the school. My parents spoke Haida with other adults but didn't make much effort to teach me. My grandma always spoke Haida to me and I tried hard to understand but it was foreign. Now, in my present life, I know that the Haida language is the key to understanding my people. I need to learn it now and be able to pass it on to my grandchildren. I would love to speak to my mom and Elders in our language. I would learn so much about my heritage and history. It is only now I see and understand the importance of the Haida language. (Bell, 2001, pp. 8-11)

Language is a conveyor of culture. Language carries the ideas by which a nation defines itself as a people. Language gives voice to a nation's stories, its mythos. Stories are not just entertainment. Stories are power. They reflect the deepest, the most intimate perceptions, relationships, and attitudes of a people. Stories show how a people, a culture thinks. Such wonderful offerings are seldom reproduced by outsiders. Cultural insight, cultural nuance, cultural metaphor, cultural symbols, hidden subtext – give a book or film the ring of truth. Images coded with our meanings are the very things missing in most "native" writing by non-native authors. These are the very things that give stories their universal appeal, that allow true empathy and shared emotion. (Slapin & Seale, 1992, pp. 98-99)

One way to develop a positive self-worth is through the wonderful art of storytelling; using First Nations stories as a pedagogical bridge allows First Nations children to understand their identity and heritage. There is a shared body of understanding among many indigenous peoples that education is really about helping an individual find his or her face, which means finding out who you are, where you come from and your unique character. (Cajete, 2000, p. 183) I believe students can build their self-confidence and self-esteem through the art of storytelling and reading.

As an educator, I believe storytelling and reading will plant seeds in the child's learning process and understanding of their unique identity. Through storytelling they will gain pride and respect for themselves. When children learn to read and write properly, they can comprehend the daily school assignments and feel proud of their accomplishments. They will be able to achieve their goals and dreams and they will be successful in completing their educational pursuits. I think I have a lot to contribute to students, regardless of their age or grade, because I am genuinely concerned about our culture. I think I've got a really good rapport with the students. They see me as a native person, and come up to me automatically. It's just easier for them to approach me because I am native. They don't have any second thoughts. I can understand their environment: where they come from. I can feel some of the struggles that their parents went through, and after I get to know them, I can help out more. If there's a problem with anything – health, lack of food – I can easily talk to them. I guess there is automatic sensitivity to me. They are able to see who I am, that I am a teacher, and that I can help them. (P. Collison as cited in Benyon, 2008, p. 11) My experiences illustrate a central principle of the landmark policy document *Indian Control of Indian Education* (1972), mainly that "[Indian] teachers . . . who have an intimate understanding of Indian traditions, psychology, way of life and language . . . are best able to create the learning environment suited to the habits and interests of the Indian child" (National Indian Brotherhood, 1972, as cited in Beynon, 2008, p. 11).

My book offers an appreciation and understanding of Haida culture and history of the *Tsath Lanas* Eagle clan through my stories and through my mother's authentic life history. I encourage other First Nations people to write their stories, through their personal experiences and eyewitness accounts, or write the stories of their Elders and grandparents. Volume VII of the *En'owkin Journal of First North American Peoples*, edited by Kateri Akiwenzie-Damm and Jeannete Armstrong, entitled *Gatherings* wrote a strong message of encouragement to Indigenous writers to be proud of who they are and to continue to tell their stories. I agree with their sentiments, for I am a Haida woman and our Indigenous voices need to be heard. The following excerpts express this powerful statement:

> indigenous writers. this is the ground upon which we stand. we know this ground and this ground knows us. she recognizes our ancestors in you. she knows our genealogy. we carry this knowing. and so we will not be moved. we will not be muted. even if our stories are ignored. no matter how many times the maps have changed, the borders shifted, the lines drawn. we will not be moved.
>
> indigenous writers this is the ground upon which we stand. this is the motherland. the gathering place. the place for remembering, for singing, for telling stories, for honoring the ones of our ancestors. this is why we stand firm. why we will not be moved. why our writing is resistance. and protest. our sacred places, our homelands, our memories are in our words.

> indigenous writers. every mark on every page is a foot firmly planted. every story, every poem, every word given breath, is eternal. imprinted into eternity. like the moon in the night sky, enduring.
>
> indigenous writers. this is our territory. this is indigenous land. where our values, our ways of speaking, our oral traditions, our languages, our philosophies, our concepts, our histories, our literary traditions, our aesthetics are expressed and accepted and honored each according to our nations. this is where we carve our stories into the memories of our people, we sing our songs our children will remember. it is to them we speak. it is for them we sing.
>
> these are our stories, our songs, our words, spoken in our voices in our ways for our people. (Akiwenzie-Damm, 1996, pp. 1-2)

The greatest contributions to academia my book offers is a First Nations woman's perspective. As an *insider,* I know what it means to be born and raised as a Haida – to live the life of a Haida. The culture, traditions and language that I learned are my culture and I want to share this vast knowledge with others, so others can gain an appreciation of our culture through my voice. Storytelling is a universal activity and may well be the oldest of the arts. It has always provided a vehicle for the expression of ideas, particularly in societies relying on oral traditions (Cruikshank, 1995, p. ix). When native peoples are allowed to speak of their history and their lives, it will be to tell the truth (Slapin & Seale, 1992, p. 13).

For many Native Americans, daily life was a process of learning with the ultimate purpose of preparing children to be functional members of their community (Tafoya, 1989, p. 40). The children learned their roles, their societal responsibilities, survival skills, artistic skills (such as carving and weaving), their histories, and tribal stories – all of which they themselves would, after the completion of their apprenticeship, pass on as they became parents and elders themselves (Stairs, 1993, p. 87). The oral traditions, the most dominant cultural tradition among Native North American communities, instilled children with tribal histories and stories in both community dwelling places and natural settings. Much of the apprenticeship for the Haida, especially concerning survival skills, involved learning about their environment. Both boys and girls received most of their practical learning out in the open air, in the forests, on the beaches, and wherever they needed to be to learn a particular skill being taught (see Blackman, 1982; Friesen, Archibald, & Jack, 1992). Within this informal learning environment, the main "teachers" were usually family members, and the content had a functional purpose to ensure survival and to preserve the tribe's oral history through stories and songs (White, 2008, p. 5).

The greatest mentors I had were my grandparents and my mother. My first teacher was my grandmother, Amanda Edgars, whom we called *Nonny*. She started intentionally teaching me the Haida culture when I was twelve years old, shortly after our house burned down in Old Massett Village. Our family went to live with our grandparents and *Nonny* Amanda taught me through observation and practice. This was the beginning of my valuable tutelage under my grandmother. Throughout my teenage and adolescent years, I always made time to visit my grandmother and listen to her tell me stories of our history and culture. My grandmother's teaching is an example of the Mission Statement found in the National Indian Brotherhoods' 1972 treatise on Indian philosophy of education:

> We want education to provide the setting in which our children can develop the fundamental attitudes and values which have an honored place in Indian tradition and culture. The values which we want to pass on to our children, values which make our people a great race, are not written in any book. They are

> found in our history, in our legends and in the culture. We believe that if an Indian child is fully aware of the important Indian values he will have reason to be proud of our race and of himself as an Indian. We want the behavior of our children to be shaped by those values which are most esteemed in our culture. When our children come to school they have already developed certain attitudes and habits which are based on experiences in the family. School programs which are influenced by these values respect cultural priority and are an extension of the education which parents give children from their first years. These early lessons emphasize attitudes of self-reliance, respect for personal freedom, generosity, respect for nature and wisdom. (as cited in Kirkness, 1992, p. 28)

As Cajete (2000) put it: "education should also help you to find your heart, which is that passionate sense of self that motivates you and moves you along in life" (as cited in Beynon, 2008, p. 53).

The Haida people had a highly structured community before the Europeans arrived in North America. Education was central for all First Nations communities. The extended families shared the responsibilities for educating and guiding the children (see White, 2008). Jeannette Armstrong (1987) describes the traditional indigenous peoples' view of education as, "a natural process occurring during everyday activities ... ensuring cultural continuity and survival of the mental, spiritual, emotional and physical well-being of the cultural unit and of its environment" (p. 14). The uncles of each family were the key teachers who guided and developed the talents of their nephews. Haida women were held in high esteem and the matriarchs of each family were the key advisors to the Chiefs. Elders were also knowledgeable about geography, subsistence, and important social values. This knowledge positioned them as respected healers, religious practitioners, historians, genealogists, and "cultural professors" (see Beynon, 2008; Sterling, 2002). My grandmother, the Late Amanda Edgars said the following: "The Haida people were powerful warriors, great protectors of the land, excellent canoe builders, and skilled and talented carvers. Each Haida Clan lived under the guidance of their Chiefs. Our people all knew which clan they belonged to, who their relatives were and what their Haida names were. They knew the stories of our people" (Edgars, personal communication, 1985).

Our Haida ancestors had a brilliant and sophisticated way of life before non-natives came to Haida Gwaii. Verna J. Kirkness's (1992) description of the traditional forms of education perfectly captures the elegance of this way of teaching:

> Long before Europeans arrived in North America, Indians had evolved their own form of education. It was an education in which the community and the natural environment were the classroom, and the land was seen as the mother of the people. Members of the community were the teachers, and each adult was responsible for ensuring that each child learned how to live a good life. The development of the whole person was emphasized through teachings which were often shared in storytelling. (p. 5)

Before contact with non-natives, First Nations and the Haida people's traditional education was linked with economics, the land, and survival. As a young girl, my grandmother taught me how to respect the land. She said: "The land is your survival. The sea will give you salmon, seaweed, clams, cockles, and many other sea foods. The trees will provide the roots for our people to weave the hats, baskets, and clothing. You have to watch, listen, and learn from the Elders to respect the land and take only enough to feed your family and share with others. When you take too much, you are not respecting the land or the food which it provides." (Edgars, 1985)

David Suzuki states the following: "North America, to the native people living here, is more than simply a place, a piece of turf. Land embodies culture, history, and the remains of distant ancestors. Land is the source of all life and the basis of identity. Land is sacred. An overriding sense in aboriginal perceptions is that of gratitude for nature's bounty and beauty. Gratitude and respect" (as cited in Henley, 1989, p. 11).

As a teacher, I believe when students are provided relevant stories, the art of storytelling and the ability to read can be used as a key strategy for First Nations and Haida children to gain respect for themselves and gain a sense of pride in their identity. As an educator, I believe a person is never too young or too old to learn. Everyday a person is able to learn something new by observation, listening, or reading. My husband attended Residential School. During the healing he needed after this experience, he found that learning from Elders and reading encouraging books helped him immeasurably. He states the following:

> Elders were a major influence in my healing process. They gave me advice and direction and helped me adjust to a more positive way of living. Uncle Herman Price, in particular, gave me many words of advice. He would always ask me how I was doing at the logging camp. I would tell him that I liked the job, but I was afraid of making mistakes. He said, "Making a mistake is what education is all about. From your mistakes you learn to never do it again and you can make improvements from your mistakes." The many years that I worked at the different logging camps gave me the time that I needed to do soul searching. My main source of education was obtained by reading. I avidly read newspapers and many books on self-improvement and religion (A. Collison, 1993, p. 39).

Through transformation stories children learn traditional values such as humility, honesty, courage, kindness, and respect.

On the Northwest Coast, each tribe has stories told of their legendary heroes. For example: Haida people and other First Nations people have stories about the Raven who was both a trickster and a creator. The Bear is the spiritual protector for the *Tsath Lanas* clan. Each clan has their own crests with special significance; the humming bird, which represents a sign of good luck to some clans, is another example of such symbols.

My grandmother has told me stories all my life, and she always gave me advice. No matter what else she told me, she always said the most important element is to listen. This oral tradition has always been one of the primary skills. We had to learn how to listen. *Nonny* said, "You have to 'listen' to what I am telling you. Don't let your emotions speak." One of the lessons I learned through my experience is the power of words. It all depends on how a person speaks to you and how you are able to use words in a positive or negative manner. In person to person interaction, indicators of the message include body language, facial expression, tone behind the words, and words themselves (Mussell, Nicholls, & Adler, 1991, p. 84).

Even in difficult circumstances, we often find the tools for change in the oppressive systems themselves. As Holland, Lachicotte, Skinner, and Cain (1998) put it: "while 'alien' voices may position us, they also provide us with tools to reshape our positions" (p. 45). In conversations, we may struggle with the positions others attempt to impose upon us. Afraid of being shot down by louder or more dominant voices, we may not say what we really think. In contrast, stories are a medium through which we may both select the positions we occupy and challenge the positions assigned to us by others. We can say what we think and feel, work out our ideas and concerns, and choose to share these if we wish. (Beynon, 2008, p. 22) It is not only through dialogue but also through story that we make sense of our own and other's lives: "In telling a fragment of his or her autobiography a speaker assigns parts and characters in the episodes described" (Davies & Harre, 1999, p. 3). During the past eighteen years of my teaching career in British Columbia,

I experienced both positive and negative encounters. Majority of my teaching experiences are positive and rewarding. It was only during several difficult encounters that I experienced in my teaching career and life that I was inspired to write the poem called "Trails and Tribulations." Learning is a lifelong process and we all live and learn something new everyday.

Through my experiences, I have learned that sometimes silence is a sign of patience, courage, and endurance. There is a time to speak and there is a time to keep silent. Haidas and everyone else have to be strong to know when it is time to speak and when it is time to refrain. *Nonny* Amanda taught me how to listen, but she also taught me when to recognize when it is time to listen to Elders and learn, and not interrupt. I was taught that silence is golden. I was taught how to listen, when to speak and when to be silent. The art of listening and knowing when to speak or not speak is another skill that I continue to learn throughout my life. Many times I reflect back to my grandmother's words of wisdom and I am grateful that I listened to her wise words. I learned that silence is regarded as the importance of character and the art of listening is the central skill and object of education. The ability to listen well and to hear all is an important objective for many Haida people. As stated by Kirkness (1992): "Although there was little segregation of family for events, whether social or work-related, children were taught that there were times when they should be silent and allow the adults to speak without interruption. Silence was regarded as the cornerstone of character. As Chief Wabasha stated, 'Guard your tongue in youth and in age you may mature a thought that will be of service to your people. The fruits of silence are self-control, true courage or endurance, patience, dignity and reverence.'" (p. 8)

I believe it is important to observe that each First Nations has developed its protocol around stories and the art of storytelling. Two other Northwest Coast communities, the Tsimshian and Nisga'a have their own protocol, which I came to understand as a member of the First Nations Council for several years (now known as the Aboriginal Council). The Nisga'a have their own protocol. Former President of the Nisga'a Tribal Council Mr. Joseph Gosnell wrote about how many years it takes to make an *adawx*. When I taught First Nations Studies 11/12, I used this newspaper article as one example to compare the difference of how the Tsimshian and Nisga'a people write their stories. In a news article called "This *adaawak* took a century to compose," Mr. Gosnell (1996) explains one example of an adawx.

> I was struck by the story of the chieftains who, more than a century ago, pushed a 50-foot cedar canoe into the Nass River and paddled down the coast to Victoria's inner harbor. They went to petition the government of the day, led by Premier William Smithe, for an early settlement to the Nisga'a Land Question. But when they reached the capitol and climbed the steps of the parliament buildings and knocked on the door they were turned away. The Nisga'a were to be turned away many times more in the decades that followed.
>
> At 8:27 a.m. Monday, a new ending was written to that long history of rejection and indifference when an agreement in principle was reached between the federal and B.C. governments and Nisga'a Tribal Council negotiators.
>
> This crucial step towards the first modern treaty in British Columbia will have positive effects far beyond the Nisga'a people, in the form of certainty, a stable climate for investment, economic development and employment.
>
> For the Nisga'a, this agreement is also significant in non-material ways; It is long-awaited acknowledgement of our dignity and our identity. It is recognition that the Nisga'a have rights to the territory our ancestors occupied and protected for thousands of

years. It breathes meaning into the guarantees of protection for aboriginal and treaty rights contained in the Canadian Constitution. It is the chance to get on with our lives, and to fashion a future as full participants in Canadian society.

For all Canadians, it is an opportunity to close the book on an unflattering chapter in the development of this country. For many years we endured laws specifically designed to destroy our language and culture and to deny our very humanity.

Until 1961, we were denied the vote. We were denied the right to put forward any claim for our land, seized without treaty or surrender. We were placed on reserves – the model for South Africa's abolished homelands under apartheid – where we were denied the right to own land or raise capital for economic development. Our cultural practices, family structure and language were nearly destroyed by anti-potlatch laws and Indian residential schools. For a time, those native people who could obtain a boat to participate in the commercial fishery were banned by law from using a motor. Slowly the discriminatory laws have been dismantled, but the original injustice against the Nisga'a remained unaddressed until the 1970s, the federal government, prompted by the Calder case, and in 1990, the provincial government began negotiations.

Critics will inevitably attack this agreement; it is already happening. Some say the governments gave away too much. Some say the Nisga'a settled for too little. I know the road ahead is not easy. It will take great resolve by political leaders to maintain a sense of history in a climate of fear-mongering and misinformation.

Certainly we did not attain everything we sought. That is the way it is with negotiations, as

> opposed to other methods of handling conflict, such as lawsuits, civil disobedience or worse.
>
> A generation of Nisga'a men and women has grown old at the negotiating table. Many more who sought a settlement, like the chieftains who voyaged to Victoria, died before they could see their dream realized.
>
> But when the *adaawx* is told to future generations, perhaps a child somewhere will hear that the canoe returned to the Nass Valley, more than a century later, carrying justice for the Nisga'a and honor for us all. (p. A23)

First Nations people of the Northwest Coast have long standing oral traditions. In my opinion, Ovide Mercredi and Bill Wilson are the most outstanding First Nations leaders in Canada. I admire Bill Wilson because he is an extremely articulate, strong, and outspoken leader. He is an advocate for many First Nations people. One example of Bill Wilson's powerful statements is found in Asch's 1988 title, *Home and Native Land.* For Bill Wilson of the Native Council of Canada, the principle of original sovereignty is linked to the principle of liberation that motivated Canadian involvement in the Second World War. As he states (as cited in Asch, 1988): "When the German forces occupied France, did the French people believe they didn't own the country? I sincerely doubt that there was one French person in France during the war that ever had the belief that France belonged to Germany, which is why, of course, they struggled with our assistance to liberate their country and once again take it back for themselves." Later, he adds: "So what we say is we have title and that is why we are talking to you about aboriginal rights, but we are not talking English Common Law definitions... international law definitions that have been interpreted and re-interpreted and sometimes extinguished by conquest and ceding treaties and other agreements like that. We are talking about the feeling that is inside . . . all of us as Metis, Indian and Inuit people that this country belongs to us" (p. 124). Wilson further elaborates on this point: "My whole point [is] that we must stop viewing [aboriginal rights] from the point of view of the dominant society if we are ever going to understand what the Indian people, the Inuit people and the Metis want" (pp. 29-30). The first issue, then, is whether there is a means of understanding this concept from the native point of view.

Ovide Mercredi mentions the concept of repetition in the book called *In The Rapids.* The Haida people passed on their history through storytelling and the Elders continuously reiterate our history, names, territories, beliefs, culture, and traditions through oratory at the potlatch ceremonies. Sometimes the Elders repeated themselves many times. In my book, I often go over a story or advice given to me by our Elders. This is how we learn through constant repetition. In the introduction of *In the Rapids*, Mary Ellen Turpel and Ovide Mercredi (1993) state the following:

> For the First Nations people, history and spirituality are not written down in the sense of a book like the Bible – they are said to be written on the hearts and passed along through storytelling, repetition and oratory. One thing most people realize almost instantly about First Nations leaders is that they are superb orators, especially when speaking in their own languages. These skills come naturally to First Nations peoples and we have many great speakers and leaders. In a reflection of the oral tradition – a tradition passed down as the backbone of First Nations knowledge, discourse and sincerity – many of the words in this book began as speeches. (pp. 10-11)

Mercredi has positive, powerful strength and I believe he is a dynamic effective Leader for the First Nations people. He states the following:

> We dream about a Canada in which our inherent right to govern ourselves is acknowledged. About a time when we can use our own political judgment, our own free will to shape our destinies and control our own affairs. We dream about healthy communities where children will be proud to say they are First Nations peoples. You see, this is what self-government of self-determination is about for our peoples. It is about self-respect, self-esteem and the future of our distinct cultures and identities. Self-determination is a basic human right. (Mercredi & Turpel, 1993)

Stories are the verbal history of the First Nations people. There are many different types of stories. Some stories are told about eyewitness accounts and testimonials. Each story may range from sacred to historical events to present day events. Each story teaches the social events of the Haida people and the political events and structure of the Hereditary Chiefs' roles. Each story teaches the traditional and cultural ways of the native way of life (National Indian Brotherhood, 1972). In my book, I tell family myths that explain our family history and stories about the sea animals and other creatures that change into human form. One example is how the Haida man who changed into a whale to provide food for his family. Another is how the Haida warrior put on the cloak of the bear to learn how to respect the bear. The bear taught the clan at Naden Harbour how to use the bear's medicine. In the teachers' guide The *Queen Charlotte Islands Reading* (Adams & Markowsky, 1985) series, Dawn Adams writes about two types of legends and beliefs:

> There were two types of legends. The first type known and told by everyone, explained how the world and its beings became as they are today. The second types were family myths that explained the

origins of family crests and sometimes the family history. These myths accounted for the high standing of the family and its right to use certain names, crests, dances and possessions.

The Haida believed that the world was inhabited by supernatural beings far more powerful than humans. The highest of them all was "Power of the Shining Heavens" who gave power to all things. All creatures were divided into sea creatures, land creatures and air creatures. In each category the members were arranged hierarchically with Killer Whale being the chief of the sea. Bear being chief of the land and Eagle being chief of the sky.

Animals were thought to possess the same type of souls as humans and to live in villages just like the Haida people. They had their own territories, chiefs and social structures. There were Salmon-people, Herring-people, Raven-people, Eagle-people, Bear-people, Killer Whale-people and many more.

Many of these creatures were believed to be capable of changing into human form at will. In their villages they lived in human form; when they wished to appear in animal form they donned cloaks, masks or skins. These supernatural beings could take humans into their villages, marry them and help or harm them. They could also give themselves as food to humans and regenerate themselves and return to their villages, provided that all their bones were returned with grace and ceremony to the environment. Humans could gain power from the spirits and by putting on skins could become that creature.

A deep respect for the spirits of all living things pervaded the daily life and work of the Haida people. Not all animals were supernatural beings in disguise, but they were respected nevertheless for their natural grace, knowledge and life-giving potential. The Haida

> recognized that each animal had some ability superior of that of humans, be it speed, cunning, strength or endurance. Before taking a salmon from the water, or bark from a tree, a person would ask permission from its spirit by giving prayers and offerings.
>
> The chief mythological character along the entire Northwest Coast was Raven. He had unlimited magical powers, an insatiable appetite and used all kinds of trickery in order to satisfy his greed. His inquisitive nature and constant bragging continually got him in trouble. He usually managed to get himself out of difficulty without any serious consequences, but while doing so, he altered various features of nature. In this way Raven created natural phenomena such as light, fire, tides and the great flood. He had to be treated with great respect because of his unpredictability.
>
> These mythological and animal crest symbols embellished everything; totem poles, canoes, houses, paddles, bowls, masks, household objects and clothing. (p. 28)

Throughout my life, I have been told many different stories. Some stories are told as a personal life history experience similar to the story told by my mother. Some stories are told for fun. Some stories are owned by a specific clan, house or family while other stories are public domain. Stories have many different purposes. Stories teach children how to survive as human beings and teach them to learn how to respect themselves before they are able to respect others. They also teach children the traditional values of sharing, caring, compassion, and understanding. Often stories are told over and over. Each time the children hear the stories, they are able to derive new meaning. It is vital that all the children are taught who they are, where they come from, and which clan they belong to. Stories were told to teach me proper behavior. Often when I was a little girl, my parents and grandmother would see what I did wrong. They did not scorn me or punish me. Instead, my father or grandmother told me a story so I could avoid making mistakes and avoid certain problems. The stories gave me some answers and made me think about what I did. Often I implemented problem-solving skills to overcome the problems I encountered. However, many times as a young girl and as an adult I made mistakes, but I learned never to make the same mistake again.

When children did wrong, the first thing we did was to provide examples of their behavior and give the children an opportunity to make better choices. We use the power of storytelling to show the right way. If children were disobedient, rude to an Elder or doing things, which might be dangerous to themselves, then they would be told one or more lesson stories designed to show what happens to those who misbehave. I think it is no exaggeration to say that all American Indian stories, when used in the right context, can serve as lesson stories and as important tools of communication (Slapin & Seale, 1987, p. 94).

Nonny Amanda told me stories I did not understand. She often told me the same story over, which is a consistent pedagogy based on repetition theory. As I grew older, I derived different meanings from her stories as I became more mature. I made new meanings and realized that those stories have various applications and understandings. Julie Cruikshank (1995) describes the listener's integral role in making a story meaningful: "Storytelling does not occur in a vacuum. Storytellers need an audience, a response, in order to make the telling a worthwhile experience" (p. 16). *Nonny* Amanda told her whole family many stories when they were young children. My mother, Gertie White, remembers the process to be similar when *Nonny* told her stories. She said,

> I remember when mom used to tell me stories. Sometimes I didn't understand some of the stories, but now that I'm older and wiser, I think back to

> when mom used to tell us stories. Now I understand what she was talking about, maybe because I'm older and I have my own children and grandchildren. Sometimes it takes a long time to finally understand some of the stories or advice our parents gave to us. This is how we learn. We learn through our own experiences and then we are able to understand many things our parents told us when we were young. (White, personal communications, 2006)

I have retold the stories *Nonny* told me about the *Haida Chief Who Built an Island, The Raven and the Moon,* and the story of the *Tow and Tow-Ustahsin.* The familiar landmark of *Tow* Hill rises several hundred feet into the air from the sands of North Beach. Geologists call *Tow* a volcanic intrusion; the Haida say he has a brother up Masset Inlet with whom he quarreled and that is why he stands alone now at the eastern extremity of the Islands. (Blackman, 1982, p. 10) I have kept the context of these stories in the storyteller's character. The purpose for retelling these stories with characters is to utilize these stories in the classroom. I often add in the characters for students to use in readers' theatre or drama classes.

Although some of the stories convey beliefs that are frightening or even humorous, our Elders also told us stories from childhood that taught us powerful beliefs. Art Collison (1993) talks about one such powerful story that he learned from his parents:

> They encouraged me to maintain the Haida customs. One of the beliefs of the Haida is about the *Sloogoo.* An animal that has a very powerful mind which can actually change itself into human form to tempt or taunt you. When my mother told me about the *Sloogoo,* I went, on my own initiative, to conquer my fears. I was fourteen years old then. I went to Kumdus slough and camped by the water's edge. My

> main goal was to conquer my fears of the wilderness and to learn about survival, as this is very important in our culture. On this particular solo trip, I was anchored along the beach at Kumdus in Masset Inlet, and as I lay in silence, I could hear paddles dipping quietly into the water. My immediate thoughts were that they may be spirits of restless Haidas paddling along the seashore. But as I watched the shadowy figures approaching closer and closer, I was surprised to see Paul White, my future father-in-law, and Victor Thompson, both strong Haida men, who were out hunting. They asked me what I was doing and I told them that I was hunting and learning how to survive on my own. (p. 40)

All the stories I have written about were told to me by my grandmother and mother. These stories represent who I am as a *Tsath Lanas* Haida woman. In the story about button blankets, I write a brief history about the importance and significance of button blankets, and I describe how to make a button blanket for teachers to use in the classroom. Often when teaching a First Nations unit, I could not find complete resources to teach specific topics, so I have included a variety of activities to do when a teacher introduces the button blanket units to students. These activities are only one component or core unit of teaching a First Nations unit. It is essential that Canadian children of every racial origin have the opportunity during their school days to learn about the history, customs, and culture of this country's original inhabitants and first citizens. We propose that education authorities, especially those in Ministries of Education should provide for this in the curricula and texts that are chosen for use in Canadian schools. (National Indian Brotherhood, 1972, pp. 1-2)

When I was recording my mother's authentic stories, I would tape her every opportunity I could when she came to visit me in Prince Rupert. Her story is about her personal experiences of her life. I did not edit her story into Standard English because it is important to capture the essence of my mother's story in her own words. I used the Socratic Method to generate many different questions I wanted to ask my mother. This approach gives her the opportunity to think about the questions and compile her thoughts before I started taping her. When Cruikshank (1995) wrote life stories of three Yukon Native Elders, she noted that "often it was difficult for her to remember the name of a place until she actually saw it again, and naming those places had the mnemonic effect of recalling events that had occurred there" (p. 25). In the beginning, it would take mom a long time to think about specific details. She would confess she has too many different stories to tell and too many songs in her mind. She needed time to think about specific details.

I taped her for a period of two years including whenever I went home to Haida Gwaii. In parts of the story, she referred to the present day. One example is when she went to the hospital in Prince Rupert to check her broken ribs. I taped her story during that period of time and mom refers to that specific incident. I believe it is important to tell my mother's personal experiences because this is part of her legacy. My mother's life history is a testimony that is an important gift for my family and Haida people. Phillips (1973) states that "the life history is still the most cognitively rich and humanly understandable way of getting at an inner view of culture. [No other type of study] can equal the life history in demonstrating what the native himself considers to be important in his own experience and how he thinks and feels about that experience" (p. 201).

Everyday, I continue to learn from my grandmother and mother's testimony through their individual narratives and personal experiences. Ethel Dassow highlights the importance of keeping our culture alive:

> The myths and legends were told and retold at potlatches, less formal gatherings, as family pastimes,

> even as bedtime stories. But their entertainment value was secondary. Here, as elsewhere, the important function of myth and legend was to pass the knowledge of traditions, morals and mores from the old to the young, maintain social cohesion and continuity, keep the culture alive and flourishing. Even today, though these people have been literate for generations and have entered mainstream culture, they keep the art of storytelling alive. (as cited in Beck, 1989, p. ix)

My mother has reinforced and validated many of the stories told by her mother, the Late Amanda Edgars. In all the stories I have written about my grandmother, I have consistently consulted with my mother to clarify, approve, and proofread my stories. She is my most valuable resource and informant in providing me with detailed information and translation of songs from the Haida language into the English language. I have made a personal decision to print the Haida words just the way they sound from my point of view. I choose not to use the International Phonetic Alphabet for personal reasons.

In the story called "My Precious Children," I mention how my grandmother used devil's club to cure *Kaakuns*; however, I did not mention how to prepare the devil's club. This beautiful and powerful shrub, with its large leaves and spiny stalks, has numerous medicinal applications for the Haida as for most other First Nations whose territories fall within its range (Turner, 2004). In addition, however, and perhaps most importantly, it was used in both ancient and contemporary contexts for its role as a protective agent and a plant which is able to bestow power and strength to an individual who understands it and uses it with respect. There are many stories in which devil's club is portrayed as a supernatural power-giver. Turner adds that "perhaps because of the special protective properties of its sharp spines, devil's club is important for protection against evil and illness. Lengths of stem can be placed above a doorway or under one's mattress, or in the four corners of a room, to protect the members of a household and keep them safe" (pp. 62, 153).

The story about *Kaakuns* is only one example of how we use devil's club. I did not include the instructions to make the medicine because the Elders taught us how to respect the medicine, and they do not want this medicine or other medicinal herbs we use to be exploited or used in an inappropriate way. Traditional medicines have been used by the Haida under strictly controlled conditions and administered by skilled practitioners having the knowledge and experience of many generations behind them. The context in which such medicines are taken can be a critical factor: diet, lifestyle, and physical and mental condition all affect the ways in which people respond to applications of medicine. Spiritual relationships of Haida with plants, including medicinal applications, are private knowledge and therefore the details of this aspect of Haida ethnobotany are not presented here. Each individual has her or his own particular connection with nature. It is important for all of us to understand that this relationship exists and that it has a profound influence on the way traditionally trained Haida perceive their lands, but equally important to respect its sacredness and essentially private nature. (Turner, 2004, pp. 21, 72)

There are several different ways to spell our clan name. In my book I spell our clan name *Tsath Lanas.* Another way to spell our clan name is *T'sath 7laanaas* or *Jath- lon-us.* I have used a few Haida vocabulary in my book; therefore, I have also included a glossary. The intricate detailed illustrations of all the Haida designs are drawn by my brother Paul White Jr. He has an incredible collection of all his silk screens and he agreed to let me use his art work in my book. The illustrations demonstrate his talented gift as a Haida artist.

There is some repetition in my mother's personal story and "The Greatest Mentor in My Life, My Dear Precious Grandmother." When there is repetition in these stories, it reinforces how the stories have been passed down from each generation to generation. I first published the story of my grandmother in the book called *Gatherings, Volume VII, the En'owkin Journal of First North American Peoples.* In this book, I have added more details and information to this specific story.

Through the art of storytelling, I was able to build links to our culture and to our past history. My goal has always been to record the stories told to me by my grandmother and to publish these stories in her honor. This book of treasurers contains three generations of stories by my grandmother, my mother, and I. It is important to note there have been some people that have passed away during the time my mother was recording her stories for me. I relay my personal condolences to the families. My mother mentioned their names in the utmost respect.

This book is a labor of love and I want to share these stories with the *Tsath Lanas* Eagle Clan, First Nations people, educators, non-native people, and my family. As an educator, I know the teachers, parents, and children will use the wonderful art of storytelling in their daily teaching and learning to motivate the children to be better readers and gain pride in their identity as First Nations children. I am confident that through this method of storytelling and reading, the First Nations children will become self-motivated to learn their language and culture. My hope is that this book will create a better understanding and appreciation of Haida heritage through the art of storytelling.

Eagle Design

The Greatest Mentor In My Life, My Dear Precious Grandmother

Nonny Amanda Edgars was my first teacher. She inspired and encouraged me to go on a spiritual journey to fulfill myself as a Haida woman by understanding our culture, history and traditions. She taught me the old ways and shared her knowledge and wisdom through the wonderful art of storytelling and artistic skills. This is the beginning of my spiritual journey. This will be a lifelong journey because learning is a lifelong process. This is a story about the greatest mentor in my life.

My name is Pansy Collison. My Haida name is Oolong-kuth-way. The Haida interpretation for my name means "Shining Gold." This name was given to me by my late Grandmother, Amanda Edgars. She was the greatest teacher and mentor in my life. In the Haida language, we call our grandmothers *Nonny*. Since I was a young girl, *Nonny* Amanda has been teaching me the Haida songs, language, traditions, and culture. She was the matriarch for our family. She knew all the Haida names for various families, and she was full of knowledge about the stories, legends, and traditions of the Haida people. *Nonny* was always willing to teach anyone who was willing to learn the Haida culture. I am very fortunate that I took the time to listen and learn the stories from the most wonderful and precious Haida teacher I've had in my life.

Nonny Amanda was born at Kung, Naden Harbour. She was born March 10, 1904. Her Haida name is Walth-ul-can-us, which means "a lady with much knowledge" in English. This name is indeed appropriate for my grandmother because she was filled with the knowledge of Haida history and traditions. She had two sisters and one brother. Her sisters' names are Mary Bell (born 1911) and Minnie Edgars (born 1915). Her late brother's name was Ambrose Bell (born 1913). *Nonny*'s mother's name was Kate Bell and her grandparents' names were Mary Guulay Bell and John Gaayaa Bell (born 1847). Mary Bell had five sons and three daughters.

Nonny Amanda is from the Eagle Clan. She originally comes from Kung. She was the oldest niece; therefore, she was passed the traditional territory of all the land on Kung and Salmon River. In 1934 she put on a house dinner and invited all the Chiefs and Elders to announce she was keeping the land in her name until the Jath-lon-us (*Tsath Lanas*) people picked a Chief. *Nonny* explained it was important to pick a Head Chief who is leader for the Clan and Chief for the territorial land of Kung and Salmon River. *Nonny* Amanda's people also came from Jath, which is located on Langara Island. She was the matriarch for the Jath-lon-us (*Tsath Lanas*) tribe because she knew all the Haida names for different families and clans. She knew the family background and the crests of many families. Many Haida people came to *Nonny* for advice and direction or simply for information. She was a very knowledgeable and respectable lady. She knew how to speak the "old" Haida language and she knew many Haida legends and stories about lands, territories, customs, and traditions.

She was married in the traditional Haida custom way. In the Haida custom a person from the Eagle Clan cannot marry a member of another Eagle Clan. The only time this is acknowledged is when the male person gets adopted to the opposite clan. *Nonny* Amanda's uncles, Phillip, John, Peter, Frank, and Louis Bell chose her husband. Her husband's name was Isaac Edgars (born 1902). In the Haida language, we call our grandfathers *Chinny*. *Chinny* Isaac was from the Raven clan. He was originally from Yan Village, which is located directly across from Old Massett Village. *Chinny* Isaac had three brothers and one sister. Their names are Joe Edgars, Timothy Edgars, and Jimmy Edgars and his sister's name was Irene Edwards.

When I was about twelve years old, our house burned down, and we had no other place to live until our house was rebuilt. This is when we moved into my Grandparent's house and I started learning about the Haida culture and language. *Nonny* would tell me stories about when she was growing up. She said that when she was a young girl she traveled all over the Queen Charlotte Islands with her parents and grandparents. They traveled with the seasons and harvested and stored foods for the winter. She remembered when they camped at Tow Hill to dig clams. They would dry the clams on sticks and they would have rows and rows of clams drying in the sun. Her parents and grandparents worked at Naden. When the work was finished at Naden, they traveled to North Island and went up the Inlet to work at Shannon Bay. During the summer they would salt salmon and dry salmon. They also picked an abundance of berries which were dried or canned in jars. In the month of October they smoked deer meat. In late April, the whole family went on a boat across to Yan Village to pick seaweed. *Nonny* said they would pack a gigantic picnic basket full of food. The whole family and many other Haida people camped at Yan Village to pick seaweed. They dried most of the seaweed on huge rocks and half dried the rest of the seaweed and then packed them into boxes. *Nonny* recalled that, "This was a fun time," when all the kids worked together and picked seaweed. Then all the children played together, and the adults sat around the fire and told stories. This was an enjoyable time when the children played and the other families shared their food. *Nonny* said that during those days, everyone would get together after they had enough food supply for the winter and they would have a potlatch. She said the Jath-lon-us (*Tsath Lanas*) family would pack baskets of food to one camp and different families took turns providing the food for the potlatch. As she reflected back to her younger days, she said "Everything was so good. Everyone shared and helped one another during those days."

As I grew older into the adolescent years, I realized that *Nonny* was teaching me many traditional values and Haida customs by telling me different stories and legends. This was how she was brought up by her mother, uncles, and grandparents. She said the Haida people did not write anything down on paper. The stories, legends, customs, and traditions were taught in an oral tradition. *Nonny* said, "The Haida people always explained their family lineage and family names in a potlatch, so everyone present in the potlatch will know their names and which territory or land belonged to them. The people present were the witnesses of Chiefs, as well as adoptions, crests and songs of families, and ownership of various land and territories. This is how the history was recorded; it was etched in the minds of all the people, so they can remember the history and pass it on to their own children and grandchildren."

Nonny Amanda was an extremely gifted and talented woman. *Nonny* knew how to weave hats and baskets out of cedar bark. She also knew how to crochet jackets, blankets, and vests. She used buffalo wool to crochet jackets and she also used the fine crochet cotton to crochet beautiful table spreads. I remember I was a teenager when she started to teach me how to crochet. It didn't take too long to learn because I would sit and watch her crochet for a while and then I would copy her.

Nonny always said, "It is important to listen and it is important to watch." I realized when she was teaching me how to crochet that listening and watching were two important skills which were to become very important elements in my daily life. As a teacher, it is important that I listen to the concerns of my students, the advice and knowledge of other teachers, and to the wisdom of the Elders. I became a very observant person by watching others. Often, I analyze different situations before I speak. I also use these skills to observe the students I am presently teaching.

I eventually learned how to crochet many different items such as bedspreads, baby blankets, baby clothes, and tissue covers. One of the most important lessons *Nonny* taught me about making button blankets or regalia is "Always put the eye part on last. In our family clan, we believe that when we put the eye part on last, the Eagle (or whatever design) will open up its eyes and thank us for keeping our history and traditions alive." When I teach the wonderful art of button blanket making, I always teach the history of the blanket making and how the Haidas make the colors red, black, and white.

Nonny Amanda was a composer of Haida songs. She composed Haida songs about her life, her children and grandchildren, and about where she traveled. She was extremely knowledgeable in the songs and dances of the Haida people. In 1962, she started the dancing group called, Haida Eagle Dancers. This is how I started learning the Haida language. *Nonny* Amanda started teaching me many Haida songs. This was a very inspiring learning experience because she would sing the songs to me and then she would interpret the Haida language into English. This seemed to be a natural learning process because I enjoyed learning the Haida songs. *Nonny* said, "Songs and crests tell everyone where you come from and which territory you come from. They are important symbols of our identity. No one can sing another family's songs and no one can wear another person's crests, unless they have permission from the appropriate owners of the songs and crests. It is just like stealing, when someone else sings the songs that belong to a certain family." *Nonny* Amanda reflected back to her grandfather's days. She said they had big wars if anyone else sang their family songs or wore their family crests. She'd say very sadly, "Today is very different, some people sing any songs and put different words in them."

I became extremely motivated by my grandmother's enthusiasm to teach me the Haida songs. I made it a habit to go to visit *Nonny* everyday after school to learn the Haida songs. Some of the songs I learned were called: Welcome song, Eagle and Raven Song, Men's Strength Song, Haida Love Song, Happy Song, Grandchildren Song, and Mourning Song. I also learned many other children's songs. She also taught me some songs in the Chinook language. *Nonny* said, "Each song has a very important meaning." For example, the Grandchildren Song tells how much the people love their children and grandchildren. Words can not express this love, so they want to squeeze their children really hard to tell them how much they love them. When I first learned this song, I was about twelve years old and didn't understand the meaning of the words. Now I understand it perfectly because I have two precious children of my own. I always want to hug them really hard to show them how much I love them. Now I have the same feelings that *Nonny* had when she was surrounded by her grandchildren. The Mourning Song is a very sad song which is only sung when a loved one has passed away or when the family holds a Memorial Potlatch for the loved one. The Hunting Song also has a special meaning. The women are singing the song for the men who went out hunting. When the men are out hunting, they cannot think of their family or they will not catch any game. One of the Haida songs I really enjoy singing is called the Happy Song.

Nonny was a very energetic lady. When she was teaching the members of the Haida Eagle Dancers, she would show them how to move their feet, arms, and body. She would say, "Watch me, see how I move my feet and arms." I felt very honored to be a part of this group because *Nonny* insisted that I start singing the Haida songs right from the beginning of when the group was organized. Aunty Margaret Hewer, *Nonny* Amanda and I were the main singers and drummers. Eventually, I became the organizer for the group and we started earning our own funds to travel to different places in British Columbia. We also traveled to Germany, Hawaii, Ottawa, and various towns throughout Alaska. Every time we performed our dances and sang the Haida songs in different cities, we ensured we wore our traditional Haida regalia. We were proud to share our Haida traditions and culture. *Nonny* Amanda always said, "Stand up and be proud of who you are. Dance and show the people who you are." Her words of encouragement were truly inspiring to each member of the group and she instilled a strong sense of pride in who we are. We danced and sang to show the people that we are Haida people and that we are continuing our powerful traditions and culture. We danced and sang to show the people that our culture and language is not being lost.

This is my story about the most inspiring lady I have ever known. Today I understand how valuable my grandmother's teachings are. Now it is my duty to teach my children and the members of the Jath-lon-us (*Tsath Lanas*) families the Haida songs and dances. As I reflect back to my younger years when I went to visit my *Nonny* Amanda, I always think what a wonderful learning experience and upbringing I had. I am always grateful for making the time to listen to my grandmother and Elders. They are truly the professional teachers in our culture and language. It is through the wealth of knowledge and experience that they pass on orally that we will survive as Haida people.

I end my story by giving advice to our young Haida people and other members of the First Nations: "Listen to your Elders and learn your traditions, culture and language. We must maintain our sense of identity through our legends, stories, songs, names, territories, and languages. We must listen and learn from our Elders." (P. Collison, 1996, p. 96)

The Late Adam Bell used to say that *Nonny* comes from two lands: She was born at Kung, Naden Harbour and the *Tsath Lanas* people also come from North Island. (Langara Island). In the olden days the Haida people buried their loved ones on their territorial lands to identify the land that belongs to their clan. *Nonny* Amanda's Uncles, Peter Bell and Louis Bell, were buried at Naden Harbour to signify that the lands of Sawbull Creek, Kung, Salmon River and areas at *Duuguus* belong to the *Tsath Lanas* clan.

Nonny was married in the old traditional Haida custom. In our custom a person from the Eagle clan cannot marry a member of the same Eagle clan. The old people use to say, "If you marry a person from the same clan, it is like marrying your own brother or sister". The only time this is acknowledged or accepted is when the male person is adopted into the opposite clan. For example, when two people from an Eagle clan want to get married, it is allowed if they are from another Village or another Eagle clan. This is a long process. The families on both sides must agree with the adoption and decide who will adopt the male into the opposite clan. The feast is hosted by both families to announce the adoption. An example is my marriage to Arthur Kenneth Collison. He belongs to another Eagle clan called the *Sgajuug ahl Laanaas* clan. I come from the *Tsath Lanas* clan. In the year 1980, Adam Bell adopted Art into his Raven clan. It was a huge honor when Adam adopted Art, and for this honor, respect was shown and witnessed at the feast. Adam told the people, this adoption was done in the traditional way of the Haida people.

Throughout my life I had many other teachers. In my younger days, they included my dad, the Late Paul White Sr., the Late Eddie Jones, the Late Reverend Alfred Davidson, and the Late Fussy Marks. Each one of these precious Elders taught me in their own special and unique way. They were my true professors and teachers in the Haida language, history, legends, philosophy, traditions, and culture.

My dad was a fisherman. He was a very knowledgeable man who spoke the Haida language fluently. Dad was our protector and our inspiration, and he ceaselessly encouraged us to succeed in life. I remember when dad used to come home from his fishing trips. He always shared the salmon with the Elders, family, and friends. Many of his friends appreciated my dad's kindness in sharing the salmon. He always brought home tons of sockeye and spring salmon. Mom would clean and preserve the salmon and she would cook up a huge spring salmon for supper. Dad would say, "We are the richest people in the world. We eat like Kings and Queens." Of course, we were not rich in monetary terms, but Dad showed us that we were rich because we had food on the table and we were able to survive by living off the land and sea. We were very fortunate because we always had plenty of seafood. My dad was a very kind man, he use to say to me, "Daughter, I love you more than a million sockeye."

I remember when I had to go to Vancouver to school. Dad said, "Daughter, some people are going to be jealous of you and some people will treat you 'mean'. It doesn't matter what these people say about you. Don't answer them back because what you say to them will hurt you more." At that time, I did not understand my dad's advice, but I soon realized there are many arrogant and many selfish people in this world. Their words of criticism, false accusations, or slanderous remarks can be very damaging, humiliating, and hurtful. These lies or false accusations can cause great stress and it can hurt the body, mind, and soul. As I grew older and wiser, I realized what my dad was saying. There were many times, I answered back to some person's remarks and soon found how true Dad's advice was. Every situation is different. I soon learned we all encounter many situations when we must know whether to respond and react or to ignore other people's comments. I didn't know that was going to be the last time I would see my dad again. He died while I was attending the University of British Columbia (UBC) in Vancouver. I will always cherish my dad's advice and I know he is still protecting our family in his own special way.

Another teacher was Eddie Jones. I graduated when I was eighteen years old from Prince Rupert Senior Secondary School. I immediately went to Camosum College to obtain a certificate in Small Business Management. After I received the certificate, I returned home and I was nominated to run for a council member position on the Old Massett Band Council. I was young, energetic, ambitious, and full of ideas and suggestions on how to help our people. I was successful in getting elected to the band council and I was eager to make a "difference" in helping the Haida people. Eddie Jones spent many years on the band council and he was my consultant and advisor. He told me to ask questions when I didn't understand the issues and don't be afraid to speak up. He said, "As council members, we are not here to help our own families, we are here to speak up and help all our people." He talked about when his Uncles were on the band council, they used to get really angry when the discussions became extremely intense. In the end, they would always shake hands and leave the meetings as friends.

I spend twelve years as a council member and four years as Deputy Chief Counselor. His advice has always been embedded in my mind and I always asked questions when I did not understand policies, funding, administrative, or local issues. I used a collaborative decision-making style to participate in the operations of the band council. When we made decisions to allocate housing subsidies, it was always a major decision because we could satisfy some people in allocating a house unit, but we could not possibly satisfy everyone. It's like the saying, "damned if you do, damned if you don't."

Some of the most frustrating issues I experienced in council were the continuous cutbacks in education, language, administration, economic development and the fact that as a council member, we could not satisfy all the people all the time. There simply weren't enough jobs and there is always a shortage of housing to accommodate all the people. The major accomplishments I did were assisting in rebuilding Chief Matthews School. Throughout all these years, I always have it in my heart to work for my people, whether it is through Council of Haida Nation, Urban Haida Society, or the *Tsath Lanas* Clan. My husband and I were a dynamic team when we were protecting our lands at Naden Harbour. We worked together to enforce the laws of the *Forest Practices Code* and I wrote numerous letters to the *Queen Charlotte Islands Observer*, Council of Haida Nation, Hereditary Chiefs, and Ministry of Forests clearly stating our concerns on the mismanagement and destruction of our lands at Naden Harbour. Chief *Thasi,* Ken Edgars, Art Collison, my cousins Terry Hamilton and Aaron Edgars, and I worked together making every effort to stop the logging companies from destroying our resources, rain forests, salmon beds, sea foods, and medicinal resources. We fought to protect the graves of our ancestors at Naden Harbour. Only five of us worked together to create positive, effective changes. We had no consultants, no lawyers, but we were a dynamic team of five who worked together to protect our lands. Plus we had some positive encouragement from the Late Ernie Collison. Each time I had to go to meetings with the Ministry of Forestry, our clan paid my fare to fly back and forth to Haida Gwaii. I was the writer and one of the speakers who voiced all our concerns, as I have written and indicated in the story called "Protecting Our Land." Today we still continue to protect our territorial lands and ensure our resources are intact for our children and grandchildren.

Another advisor was Reverend Alfred Davidson. He was a long outstanding council member for the Old Massett Band Council. He was the marriage counselor for my husband and I. Reverend Davidson counseled all the couples that were going to get married. He gave each couple advice and direction in their future lives together. Alfred and his wife Rose were outstanding role models for the younger people. They both understood and spoke the Haida language fluently and they were raised in the traditional manner. They knew how to preserve Haida foods. They always had a warm friendly greeting for everyone in the community, especially for my husband. Art was always working at Naden Harbour. When he came back from work, Alfred and Rose always greeted him with love and genuine kindness. They loved him just like their own son and they treated him with great respect.

It didn't matter where we saw Alfred and Rose; whenever we saw them they were always walking together holding each other's hands. This is the vision I have of Alfred and Rose whenever I think of them. I will always remember the love they showed to my husband and many people of Haida Gwaii. Most of all, I will remember the wise words Alfred had for us before we got married. He said, "When young people get married, they have to learn to talk with one another. They have to talk about their problems and accomplishments." Uncle Alfred was right. Dialogue is vital and essential in a marriage.

I also count Uncle Fussy Marks as one of my teachers. He used to phone me up everyday and ask me how I am doing in the Haida language. We made this a daily habit to phone each other or talk whenever we saw each other. Often we went to play bingo at Port Clements, New Massett, or Skidegate. Uncle Fussy taught me a new word in our language everyday. For example, when we were driving to Skidegate or Port Clements to play bingo, he would tell me stories and teach me different Haida words. He also challenged me to make good choices and be responsible for what I do in life. He always told me different stories about when they were growing up and how different it is today. I am truly grateful for all the Haida teachers I had when I was growing up. They made a significant difference in my life.

I remember when *Nonny* and mom took some of my brothers and cousins to Blue Jacket near *Tow Hill.* Mom would drive us to Blue Jacket so we could pull the cedar roots. We would spend all day pulling roots. After we pulled enough roots for *Nonny*, we would eat a delicious lunch and snacks. Then we played on the sandy beach. This was not work. It was fun. *Nonny* and mom would sit up near the beach watching us play while they cleaned the cedar roots.

I remember we always had a chore to do everyday or we were always involved in pulling cedar roots, baking bread, chopping wood, packing water, cleaning the house, digging clams, or helping my mom clean salmon. When my mother and father were working, it was my job to cook for all my brothers and sisters. I started making bread and cooking when I was ten years old. I made homemade bread every week for our family, and it was my job to baby-sit my younger brothers and sisters. We use to pick berries around the back of the houses in the village and our whole family would go out to pick seaweed on the rocks at *Yan* Village. As long as I can remember, we always went to pick hemlock and spruce cones. I remember when my brother, Johnny was a baby, we carried him into the woods and mom laid him in a cradle while *Nonny,* Mom, and my family picked cones. Mom drove us all over to *Juskatla, Yakoun* River and all along the roads to Queen Charlotte City picking cones and filling up sacks and sacks of hemlock and spruce cones. Every time I drive by a certain place on the highway near Tlell where we picked cones, I remember how hard we worked. I can visualize *Nonny,* Mom and I picking the cones and packing the sacks of cones on our backs to the truck. Sometimes we had to carry the sacks a long way to the side of the road. That's what I call "tough" Haida women. Today's generation is so different; they get paid or receive an allowance for everything they do. My husband said, "When I was a little boy, I was lucky to get a wooden car for my Christmas gift. I had to work all day to get twenty-five cents. In those days twenty-five cents was a lot of money and I had to work really hard to get a quarter."

Nonny taught me how to listen and now I am teaching my grade one class how to listen. During the morning circle, talking tables, or during guided reading, I read a variety of stories both fiction and non-fiction to the students. I teach them the concepts of how to listen and learn. Before, during, and at the end of the story, I ask them stimulating questions for clarification and understanding. I ask students to make predictions about the stories or exchange ideas on a specific topic. The students are able to use listening to develop their thinking to make connections and utilize their background knowledge to acquire new ideas. The students provide examples both oral and written on how they learn how to listen. I teach the students how to spell the words *listen* and *learn.* Sometimes when the students are disruptive in class, I put up my hand and I ask all the students to spell the word *listen.* This method works sometimes and the students focus and work quietly to complete their work. I learned one strategy from my sponsor teacher, colleague, and friend, Della Gibson. She's a remarkable lady with a dynamic personality and a happy friendly smile.

Della and I always helped each other out in our professional teaching career, and we always shared our ideas and gave each other advice, moral support, and encouragement. In 1997, I was teaching at Roosevelt Elementary School, I remember when Della put up one hand in the air to signify this means a silent signal. This was during an assembly, she put up her hand and within a couple of minutes she had all the students from kindergarten to grade seven paying attention and listening quietly. She taught majority of the students and they indeed demonstrated the respect they have for her as a teacher.

This signal meant to be quiet and listen. When I put up my hand in my class, one observant student would say, "the silent signal." I ask the students to put up their hands when they are ready to listen. Some students may be talking and I tell them they are not ready to listen. I say "Please put your hand down; you are not ready to listen." The students learn quickly to raise their hands quietly; this indicates they are willing to be attentive and willing to learn. I love teaching the young, eager students. I believe, perhaps, that I have made a big difference in their lives and they will be good listeners and learners as they grow and mature in their daily lives.

When *Nonny* was teaching me the Haida language, she always corrected me when I mispronounced the words. The Haida language is very difficult and has many glotilized sounds. Some people put different meanings in the words and songs. An example of how some people change the meaning is a song called *Sic Dim Dolla.* The most delicate way to interpret the meaning of the song is "give me money." This song is not a Haida song. It is originally a Chinook song, but some Haida dance groups still sing this song and use a different interpretation for this song. Uncle Adam Bell told *Nonny* and the young people not to sing this song again. Today, some of the Haida language is not used appropriately. An example is a word we say in our language called *cheegun.* This word is used when a man goes to the bathroom as it means "a man standing up." Today, some women say this word, though it is proper only for men to use this word; the women have their own Haida word to say when they are going to the bathroom. This is an example of when it is absolutely necessary to listen to the Elders in how to pronounce the words appropriately and accurately.

I also learned various greetings and phrases in the *Smalgyax* language. My sister, Isabelle Lewis is my *Smalgyax* teacher. When the Tsimshian Elders talk in their language, I believe their language sounds like a melody similar to a rhythm in a song. I believe their language is easier to learn than the Haida language. When I am witnessing a feast, I can listen to the Elders talk in their language and I can understand some of the words. I also taught Isabelle the Haida language. We are both teachers and we graduated and obtained our Teacher's Certificate and Degree in General Studies at the same time from Simon Fraser University. It's rather amusing when we talk our languages. Very few people can understand us because we talk and combine both languages. I find it really humorous and rather entertaining when anyone listens to us talk in two languages. When I make a public speech at a feast, potlatch, gatherings, or political conferences, I am able to introduce myself in the Haida and *Smalgyax* languages.

I remember when my mom, *Nonny*, and I went to visit *Chinny* Isaac. He had a stroke and he couldn't talk, but when he saw us walking into the hospital, he went to his room and he started packing his clothes. He wanted to come home, but we had to leave him in the hospital for professional care. When *Chinny* Isaac died, I sang the Mourning Song. My tears were running down my cheeks. I sang this song from my heart for the kindest and gentlest man I ever knew in my entire life. This Mourning Song is only sung when a loved one goes to the spirit world. We sing this song and wear our traditional button blankets. Our clan members throw the left side of the blanket over our shoulders to signify the love and respect we have for our loved one. This same song is sung at the memorial potlatch a year or several years later when the family puts on a memorial potlatch and moves the headstone to the grave site. I sang this song for *Chinny* Isaac at the headstone moving potlatch. This time we throw the right side of the blanket over our shoulders. This signifies that we will no longer cry for our loved one. Some Haida people believe that if a person cries too much for a loved one that has passed away, their spirit will not rest in peace when they go to the spirit world.

When I sing the Hunting Song, our dance group uses carved weapons to indicate the men are going out hunting. They dance in movements to indicate they are hunting for various animals and food. The women dance behind the men, carrying a basket and button blanket to demonstrate they are supporting the hunters and waiting for them at home. Before the men go out hunting, they cleanse themselves in devil's club to give them strength and good luck.

My absolute favorite song is called the Happy Song. There are many different versions of a happy song. The song I sing means, "I'm so happy, I'm smiling from ear to ear." It also means we are happy to keep the Haida songs and traditions alive. I always sing this song at special and happy occasions. I also like to sing songs composed by Vernon Williams. He is a young remarkable composer of songs. When I go home to Haida Gwaii, I always enjoy listening to him sing and I thank him and acknowledge him for sharing all his songs with the Haida people.

The Men's Strength Song is a fast dance where all the men challenge each other to show off their strength and agility. It is exciting and a proud moment when we witness the raven and eagle men dancing in a feast or potlatch. They dance with agility and they show everyone which clan they belong to. Often some of the men challenge each other in a fun competitive style. It makes my heart flutter with pride when I witness all the Haida men dancing at a potlatch.

All my life, I have enjoyed singing Haida songs. It makes me feel happy and proud to be able to sing songs and to be able to share my knowledge with people who are willing to listen. *Nonny* said, "I will teach you and Margaret [Hewer] the Haida songs. It is important that the songs are carried onto each generation in our family." She later said, "The songs tell stories about our family lineage and where our families come from. It is important that each of you teach your children and grandchildren the songs. They will feel proud of their culture and heritage." Today, I have taken her advice and I have taught my daughter and cousins the songs. All of my brother Paul's children are sporty and active; they all have powerful voices and are always eager and proud to perform the Haida dances. My cousin Diane York is an awesome singer and leader. She has taken on the role to lead one of the dance groups in Massett and my cousin Delbert Smith is an outstanding Haida dancer. It is always a pleasure to watch him perform at a potlatch because he puts all his energy and spirit into dancing and showing everyone he is proud to be a Haida man.

Each year the All Native Tournament Committee selects a Nation to open up the All Native Tournament in Prince Rupert, B.C. When it was time for the Haida Nation to open up the tournament, I was selected to organize and coordinate a united Haida Nation dance group. This was indeed a challenging and exciting endeavor. The first priority was to contact all the leaders of the dance groups in Prince Rupert, Massett, Skidegate, Vancouver, Hydaburg and other cities in Alaska. I arranged meetings at Massett and Prince Rupert with the leaders to select the songs for the grand entrance. We put the songs on tapes so all the dance groups could practice the songs and dances in the various cities and I arranged several practices before the grand entrance at Prince Rupert Civic Center. We held meetings with the Hereditary Chiefs and arranged the appropriate protocol of who were the speakers for this grand event. The Hereditary Chiefs, wives, matriarchs, and Elders led us into the civic center. The Haida Nation dance groups were spectacular. There were over three hundred dancers, dressed in their finest and most elegant dancing regalia. The dances were impressive and persuasive, and the singers and drummers performed magnificently. It was indeed an honor to coordinate this grand Haida Nation dance group. This was made possible with the excellent team effort of the dance leaders and the guidance of the Haida Hereditary Chiefs. The dancers were awesome and there performance will be something to talk about for many years.

I enjoy teaching songs and dances to all age groups. During the years I was the leader for the Haida Eagle Dance group we traveled all over the country. We spend five weeks in Germany traveling to different cities. I remember when our dance group traveled to East Germany on a bus, we were stopped every mile by German soldiers when we passed the Berlin Wall. During our visit to East and West Germany, the people were very hospitable. They loved to watch us perform and they were extremely interested in learning our culture. We danced in front of approximately five thousand people in an open arena, with an incredible background of manmade scenery of streams, mountains and waterfalls. Every day, we went to a different city to perform and they treated us with honor and respect. When our dance group traveled to Hawaii, we participated in a huge parade on the first day we arrived. It was exciting and new experience for us, but the heat was unbearable when were walking in the parade with our heavy dance regalia. The next day, we joined in the dancing competitions and I won the women's fancy dance and my friend Maureen Brown won another women's dance competition. We witnessed different United States First Nations dance groups perform every day. It was interesting to listen to their songs and watch their fast dancing performances. The singers all sit around one huge drum and they have a very fast singing rhythm. This was another fun learning experience we had when we were traveling to different cities. *Nonny* always gave our dance group words of encouragement to dance with pride because of who we are.

Today, my support and inspiration is modelled by my Uncle Dean Edgars, *Nonny*'s son. I am grateful Uncle Dean is there for our family, to give us advice and encouragement. This is my story about the most inspiring lady I have ever known. There is one vision I always have of *Nonny* Amanda when she was teaching me. I remember when she was weaving; sewing a button blanket or crocheting table covers. It always amazed me how she was able to weave a hat, tell me stories, and smoke a cigarette all at the same time. She always rolled her own cigarettes. When her cigarette went out, she still had the cigarette hanging in her mouth and she just kept talking and telling me stories. While she was talking, her cigarette would be moving up and down in her mouth. Sometimes I can visualize my grandmother in my mind and I often think what an amazing and remarkable woman she was and I realize how much I miss her and love her. I say *how-a*, thank you, to the greatest mentor in my life. *Nonny* made me a strong and knowledgeable Haida woman. *How-a Nonny*, I love you.

Human Man

How the Haida People Were Created

The Raven is the creator for many living things. The Raven made the birds, the salmon, the plants, and many other living creatures. He stole the light from the old man who kept the light in a box. He scattered it throughout the sky to create the day and night. At night the stars shone brightly along side the moon. During the day the sun glittered its brightness upon the sandy beach, rivers and streams and all the lands of Haida Gwaii. There are many stories about the Raven. This story was told to Nonny by her great grandmother and passed on through each generation. This is the story about how the Haida people were created.

This was a time after the great flood which happened long before my great grandmother's time. There was a great flood and the flood covered the earth for many days. Finally, one day the flood lowered and the lands of Haida Gwaii soon became dry. There were miles and miles of beautiful sandy beach near a place called *Tow* Hill. The sandy beach extended all the way to Rose Spit.

In the Haida language we call the Raven, *Yehl.* The raven is a huge black bird. *Yehl* was flying over the beautiful sandy beach looking for food. The raven flew down and ate crabs along the shores of *Tow* Hill. He flew along the sandy beach to swoop up salmon to eat. Soon he was full and he didn't feel hungry anymore. He flew down to *Tow* Hill beach and began walking on the beach. As he walked along the sandy beach, he could hear the roar of the ocean as the waves splashed along the beach. He could hear the gentle wind blowing and he could see the calm blue sky. He could see the tall beautiful green cedar trees all along the stunning beach. There were white shells and beautiful agates along the shoreline and he could see the sandy beach as far as his eye could see.

Yehl walked along the sandy beaches of *Tow* Hill. As he was walking, he felt lonely. He wanted someone to talk to and play with. As he was walking along the beach, looking into the empty sky, he heard a soft strange sound. The faint sound came from inside the white sand just near his feet. To his delight, he heard another quiet bizarre sound. The Raven immediately turned toward the sounds. Suddenly a tiny hole appeared in the white sand and tiny bubbles came from the small hole. Soon more bubbles appeared and the hole became larger. To his surprise and delight, a clam shell came out of the sand and before his eyes appeared a gigantic clamshell.

Soon a little head appeared out of the clamshell. The little eyes looked up at the Raven and became afraid of the big black bird. The little human being immediately pulled his tiny head back into the clam shell. The Raven was sad and lonely. He begged the little creatures to come out of the clamshell. Raven said, "Come out, I will not hurt you. I am sad and lonely. Please come out." The little creatures heard what the Raven said, and they trusted his gentle voice. Soon the little creatures began to come out of the clamshell. One at a time. Each little creature crawled out of the clamshell and stood on the sandy beach. Each mother and father came out together, holding and protecting their children from any harm. One by one all the families came out. They looked around to see if it was safe. They came out of the clamshell and they looked into the beautiful blue sky and breathed the clean fresh air. They looked at the beautiful crashing waves along the sandy beach. They looked at the beautiful bountiful land. The little creatures looked at the large cedar trees and green grass. They could see the sea resources at their immediate reach. They smiled and they were happy. These were the original Haida people. The Haida people were born between the land and sea.

The people looked at the lands of Haida Gwaii and looked

at the green forests and sandy beaches. They said, "It is beautiful here." The Raven was happy. He taught the Haida people many clever tricks. He taught them how to respect the lands and how to hunt for food. The people protected and treated the lands, animals, salmon, waters, and trees with the greatest of respect. Soon it was time for each group of Haida people to leave in different directions. Raven stood there as he watched each family leave. One group of people went in each direction. Each group were to become known as the Eagle and Raven clans. The Eagle and Raven clans went in different directions all over the Islands of Haida Gwaii to claim their territories. All the people respected the lands each Hereditary Chief claimed for their clan.

Soon all the people left in different directions. They established their own Social structure. They established their own traditions and maintained their own culture. They protected the lands of Haida Gwaii for thousands of years. They only took enough to survive and they respected and protected the rich resources. Each clan built strong longhouses and carved their crests and history on the beautiful totem poles.

For many generations the people grew, thrived, and prospered. They fought with other clans and they fought with many different villages along the Northwest Coast. After many years of fighting, they made friends with different villages and they had intermarriages to build a strong nation. They built strong villages and displayed their family crests on house posts, totem poles, carvings, and regalia. They built a strong Nation with their own culture. Their traditions and beliefs are embedded in their stories, songs, and dances. The people lived with the constant changing seasons and rituals of their rich lives. The Raven was ecstatic and in high spirits. He knew the Haida people would flourish and live forever on the beautiful lands of Haida Gwaii.

The Haida Women and the Bears

Long ago a young girl went picking berries with her *Nonny*. They went to the edge of a village called Ki-Yung. The girl and her *Nonny* carried their spruce root baskets. After they picked the berries from several bushes, they walked further into the woods. The girl came across some bear tracks and bear's urine. The girl stepped on the bear's urine remains and started to make fun of the bear. She began to sneer and laugh at the bear. The bear was nearby and heard what the girl was saying. This made the bear very angry. He decided to teach the girl a lesson.

The bear picked up the girl and carried her far into the woods where the bears lived. The girl was held captive for many days. While she was held captive, she observed the bears. She saw how the bears treated each other with respect. She watched how the mother bears' treated their children with love and understanding. Everyday, she watched the bears show compassion and appreciation for each other's feelings. But soon, she was getting lonely for her own people and she kept thinking about different ways she could escape.

One day, she cleverly convinced the bear to let her pierce his ears. She made the bear lie down and she pierced the bear's ears. While the bear was busy attending to his ear, she was able to escape back to her own village. When she returned home, she told her people about how the bears treated each other. She taught the women and children how to appreciate the gifts from the Creator. She taught them how to carry on the cultural values and care for one another. She also taught them how to respect the gifts of nature and how to respect and care for the land. The most important lesson she learned was not to make fun of bears again.

Bears and Picking Berries

Nonny Amanda and two Haida ladies were picking berries at the edge of Kung Village in Naden Harbour. *Nonny* was born in this village and she was familiar with the surrounding areas. She knew where to pick berries, spruce roots, and collect different kinds of shrubs for Indian medicine. *Nonny* Amanda, Hannah, and Grace took a basket full of food and water. They wanted to stay in the woods until they filled all their baskets with berries.

Before they proceeded into the woods, *Nonny* said, "Put on your kerchief. We always have to put something on our heads, so the bears won't see our hair. He might mistake us for a bear". Grace, Hannah, and *Nonny* put on their kerchiefs and they went into the woods to pick berries.

Soon they were going in opposite directions, but they all knew how to keep in contact with one another. *Nonny* Amanda said, "*Whooo*" out loud. There was no reply, so she said, "*Whooo*" again. Soon there was a reply from Grace. *Nonny* could hear a distant voice answering her back. She could hear Grace saying "*Whooo.*" *Nonny* said, "This is one of the Haida signals we use when we are out in the woods. We say this sound to let each other know where we are in the woods. When they answer back, we know they are all safe."

After picking salmon berries for several hours, *Nonny* filled all her baskets with berries. In the Haida language we call the salmon berries *skou-un*. She felt happy she had filled her baskets. She started walking back to the entrance of the woods where they started their journey. While she was walking, she started to say "*Whooo.*" Grace replied back, but she did not hear a reply from Hannah. Soon Hannah came running out of the woods. She was terrified and breathing loud. She said she went to a big log. There was a big patch of berries behind the log. All of a sudden a big bear stood up on its hind legs and started growling at her. She didn't know what to do, so she spoke to the bear in a gentle voice. She said in the Haida language, "*Clun*, stop I'm picking berries. I will not hurt you." The bear seemed to understand what she was saying and the bear put his big paws down and left her alone.

Nonny Amanda and Grace were happy that Hannah was safe. They were glad she knew what to do. The bears can sense when someone is scared of them. *Nonny*, Grace, and Hannah started talking in the Haida language as they reflected on what their grandparents used to tell them. *Nonny* said, "Our grandparents told us not to make fun of the bears or animals and don't make fun of other people."

The Haida people believe that when a person makes fun of animals or when a person treats another person with disrespect or treats them in a mean or negative manner, their own selfishness will go right back to them.

Christmas Design

Chinny Benjamin

The following story is about my father's dad, Chinny Benjamin White. I did not know my Grandfather. He died before I was born. Nonny Amanda insisted it was important that I know some of the experiences Chinny Ben had when he was young. Chinny Ben was originally born in Alaska. He was born in 1871. He was married on January 21, 1896 to Martha Ridley. He was twenty-five years old. Martha was seventeen years old. The witnesses for this marriage were Flora Ridley, Mary Ridley, Emily Edenshaw, and Edith Ltilthda. My grandfather was married twice. His second wife was Eliza Taylor. He married Nonny Eliza on March 9, 1915. The witnesses for their marriage were Robert Bennett and Lily Nelson. Phillip was born in 1872. At the age of twenty-four he married Amy Edenshaw who was fifty years old. The witnesses for this marriage was Fredrick Young, Robert Gunia, and Edith Ltilthda.

Nonny Amanda told me many stories about my grandfather, His Haida name was Sk'an-now. *He is from the Eagle tribe. He had one brother named Phillip White and he had one sister. However, Nonny Amanda could not remember his sister's name because she moved to Kasaan when she was very young. These are the stories my grandmother told me about my grandfather.*

When *Chinny* Ben was very young, he went with several Haida men on a long journey. They travelled to Hawaii on very large canoes. It took them many days to travel to Hawaii. When they arrived on the Islands, they saw foot prints. They all got off the canoe to find out who was on the Islands. *Chinny* Ben said, it was the Hawaiian people. He said they stayed there for many days. One family wanted to adopt him. This Hawaiian family wanted to adopt him because he looked just like the son they had recently lost. *Nonny* remembers *Chinny* Ben saying; "They treated me very well. Everyone was very kind to me." But soon he wanted to go back home. So the Haida men started their long journey back. While they were travelling they were getting very tired. A killer whale came along side the canoe and one of the men said to the killer whale. "Take us as far as you can. When you see our land you can let us go." The killer whale understood what the man said and the killer whale pulled them as far as Haida Gwaii. The killer whale let them go and then the killer whale swam away.

Chinny Ben travelled to Japan and to the Bering Straits on enormous Haida canoes. *Chinny* Ben and the other Haida men were travelling for a long time. They were hungry and they had on dirty clothes. His socks had holes in them when he arrived in Japan. The Japanese people were excited about the men travelling in the huge magnificent canoes. They were far away from home. *Chinny* Ben wanted clean clothes. *Nonny* says *Chinny* Benjamin would chuckle when he recalls the incident about his socks. He said, "They were so nice to me. They made me take off my socks and they mended them right there, while I was sitting there". But *Chinny* Ben recalls when he got very sick during this journey. He said their resources of food supplies ran out and they had to eat lots of strange food.

They decided to return home to Haida Gwaii. It was a long journey. When they arrived in Victoria, B.C. he ate some Indian food. He ate smoked salmon, *oolican* grease, boiled potatoes, and seaweed. After he ate, the Indian food, he said he got better. They used to call Victoria *Muck-tul-lay* during those days. *Chinny* Ben used to laugh really hard because he said, he didn't know what ice cream was, but he ate it any ways. He said, "It is strange, but it is good." *Nonny* said, "Ben was a well respected man," The Haida people respected him because he travelled to Japan, Hawaii, and the Bering Straits.

These are some of the stories *Nonny* Amanda told me about my grandfather. Many Haida Elders talked about him and said he was a very well-respected man. I value their acknowledgement of my grandfather. It is through the words of the Elders and *Nonny* Amanda that I have been able to learn about my grandfather. His original name was Benjamin Edensu.

He was born in 1871. During the period in 1890 the Indian Agent changed his name to Benjamin White. The Indian Agent told my grandfather there are too many people with the Edensu name. My grandfather *Chinny* Ben died in 1948 at the age of seventy-seven years old, still bearing the name "White." In the olden days there were two ways to say the same name *Edenshaw* and *Edensu.* My dad always wanted to find his dad's brother who stayed in Hawaii and he wanted to find his dad's sister who stayed behind in Kasaan, Alaska. He said we have many relatives who we don't know and he wanted to find them while he was still alive. Perhaps this will be my mission or my destiny is to find our relatives at Kasaan and Hawaii.

I have many personal memories of my grandmother, *Nonny* Eliza White. When *Chinny* Ben died, my oldest brother Isaac White was only nine months old. During that time, Isaac was the only child of our parents, who soon were to have five sons and two daughters. My grandmother's name was Elizah White. We used to call her Big *Nonny* and we used to call my mother's mom, the Late Amanda Edgars, Small *Nonny. Nonny* Eliza was a tall, slender woman with long black hair. *Nonny* Amanda was a short and petite woman with short curly hair. Both my grandmothers were kind, wise, and elegant women. They both had a wealth of knowledge to teach all the grand-children.

Nonny Amanda is from the Eagle clan, whereas *Nonny* Eliza is from the Raven clan. Big *Nonny* lost her eye sight when she was a young woman, so she never knew how we looked. Every time Isaac and I went to visit her, she would feel our faces and talk to us in the Haida language. One day she said to me,

"You will grow up nice and healthy." Even though she was blind, she managed to go through the entire village without assistance from anyone. She was familiar with every road and trail. We lived on top of a hill and every time Isaac and I seen Big *Nonny* walking to visit her friends, we would leap up as fast as we could and run down to help *Nonny* Eliza. My dad said, "My mom has the cleanest house in the village." The reason he said this is because, his mother always kept her entire house clean. She hand scrubbed her wooden floors and she always kept her wood stove warm. Every day she chopped wood and kindling. My brother, Isaac and I always helped our grandmother.

Big *Nonny* had a huge garden in her backyard. Her house was located beside the field in Haida Village. There were bushes of raspberries, gooseberries, and salmon berries. She also had a patch of potatoes and rows of rhubarb growing in her backyard. Sometimes, my friends and I used to pick her berries. We had a grand time picking and eating berries. Many times, Big *Nonny* knew we were eating most of the berries, but she never scolded us.

When we were very young, I remember when *Super* and I went down to visit *Nonny* Eliza. She would hear our footsteps and she would recognize us. I always liked to watch her comb her long black hair. Her hair hung right to her waist. Everyday she would comb her hair and tie it into a big bun. Today, my relatives say I look just like my grandmother because I always have my hair tied back in a bun.

One time when I was sitting beside Big *Nonny*, she took my hands and gently pressed each half moon on my finger nails. She said, "*Gaa-daa*, good things will happen to you. You will do good things for our family and our people. You will be a very wealthy woman." I always think about my grandmother's words. As I reflect back to my life's experiences I know I completed many tasks and provided assistance and guidance for my family and *Tsath Lanas* clan. I have always been a strong advocate for students and I have always maintained a strong voice in the political arena. Perhaps she meant I am wealthy because I was blessed with my own children.

I often think of the wonderful times I spent with Big *Nonny.* I miss her kind welcoming voice and when I feel sad, I always remember the kind words of wisdom and knowledge she shared with me. This brings a smile to my face. I will always treasure the moments I had with both my precious grandmothers. They were indeed the backbone of strength and knowledge for our families. They are beautiful Haida women who experienced the dynamic life of the great Haidas in their generation. I believe they are both smiling down at me from the spirit world and they are giving me the strength and courage to make the right choices and help out my family and people in an honorable and respectful manner.

Pansy Collison

Stolly White

Fraser Williams, Johnny White

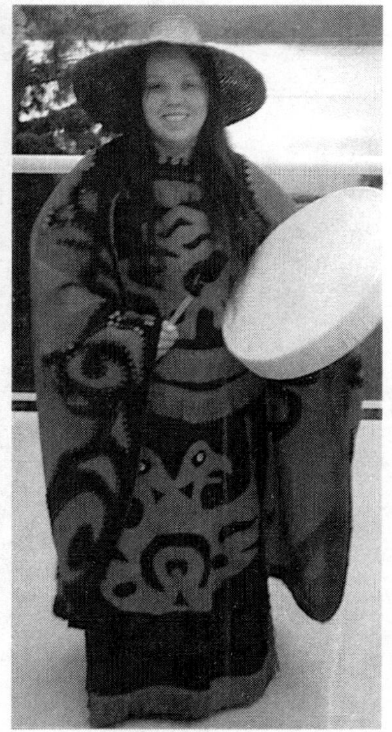

Stolly Collison

Art Collison

Gertie White and her great-grandson Lashane

Bear Pole carved by Paul White

Eagle button blanket made by Pansy Collison

(top left to right) Art Collison, Pansy Collison, Tatzen Collison, Stolly Collison; (front left to right) Gertie White, Kwiiaas Parnell

Our Precious Gifts

Stories have been part of my life since I was a young girl. I was brought up in the wonderful world of storytelling by my grandmother. Stories are like a medicine to me. It is essential food for my soul. Throughout my life, I have heard many stories about our history, culture, beliefs and traditions. Many times my grandmother told my brothers, cousins and I stories when we did something wrong. She told us stories to prevent us from making mistakes. Sometimes we made mistakes and she told us stories on how we can correct our mistakes. Nonny told us stories to educate us and often she told us the same story over and over again. Each time she told us a story, we derived a new meaning and understanding. Stories are an integral part of our culture. As Haida people, we make stories, we tell stories and we live stories. This is a story about a Haida lady named Shining Gold.

Shining Gold was born and raised on Haida Gwaii. She lived in a small community where she knew all her cousins, aunts, uncles, and grandparents. Everyday she went down to the field and played with her friends and cousins. They liked to play the game called Colors. This is a game where two teams were selected. One team hid away, while the other team looked for them. Shining Gold always had a great captain who would leave mysterious clues for the other team to find them. They used to run all over the entire village, before the other team caught up with them. This was a fun game and often there were about eight to ten people on one team. Sometimes it took the other team all day to find Shining Gold's team.

Shining Gold has five brothers and one sister. They lived in a house located on top of a hill near the church. Shining Gold always babysat her younger brothers and sister when her mother went to work at the cannery. She learned how to bake bread at a very young age. It was her job to make bread and cook when her mother was working or when her father was out fishing. Her older brother's job was to chop wood and make kindling for the wood stove and pack buckets of rain water from behind Eddie Jones's house.

Shining Gold loved to go visit her grandmother and watch her crochet blankets or weave baskets and hats out of cedar bark. She liked to watch her grandfather take care of his fishing nets or fix his boat down by the beach. But she couldn't stand going to school. Many of the children were sent out to residential school, but Shining Gold's parents did not let the Indian Agent take their children. All their children went to an Indian Day School in the village. Everyday she walked to the Indian Day School. The school was located at the end of the village. She did not like going to school and her grandmother could see how frustrated and unhappy her granddaughter was becoming every day. She asked Shining Gold why she didn't like school. Shining Gold said, "*Nonny,* I don't like to line up everyday at school and take cod-liver oil. The teacher gives us a tablespoon of cod liver oil every day. We have to eat hard biscuits and drink powdered milk. If we don't take the cod liver oil or eat the biscuits, the teacher will strap us in front of the whole class. The kids call the hard biscuits, "dog biscuits" and they taste awful. One morning, I would not let the teacher put the cod liver oil in my mouth and she got really mad at me. She yanked me in front of the class and she took out her big leather strap. She strapped both my hand knuckles really hard. No one in the classroom said a word. I didn't make a sound, but I could feel the tears running down my cheeks. The teacher straps us for no reason. If we don't sing a song, she will come over and yank us in front of the class and force us to sing. She strapped me on both my palms and then she strapped me on my knuckles. I don't like going to school. When we don't know how to do the math problems, she gets mad at us. She calls us terrible names and she hits her big ruler on the desk. Sometimes she yanks our ears really hard when we don't know how to do our work. My teacher is too mean. I don't want to go to school."

Her grandmother was very concerned about how Shining Gold was treated in school, but she told Shining Gold how important it is to get an education. *Nonny* smiled at her granddaughter. She said, "*How-wheet,* come sit by me. Let me tell you a story about the precious gifts we received from our Creator." Nonny said, "This is a story told by many Indian people. All the people have their own way of telling the story about how the Creator gave us our eyes, hands, ears, feet, heart and mind. This is a story I heard when I was a young girl. This is a good story. It will help you use your mind to learn everything at school. It is will help you use your heart to understand".

"When the Creator was putting us together as human beings, the Creator was very smart. The Creator gave us two eyes so we could see both sides of life. He gave us two eyes so we could choose our journey of life. He gave us two eyes so we could be able to see right from wrong.

"The Creator gave us two ears so we could hear out of both ears. He gave us two ears so we can hear both sides of every story. He gave us two ears so we could listen to our Elders and learn our culture and traditions.

"The Creator gave us two feet so we could walk forward in life. He gave us two feet to carry our body and walk straight and tall. He gave us two feet to walk tall and be proud of who we are as native people.

"The Creator gave us two hands to love and comfort our families and protect them from harm. We use our hands to give and to receive. We use our hands to create beautiful carvings, totem poles, canoes, and sew our regalia. Our hands have a lot of power to love or to destroy. It is up to us to use our hands in a positive way.

"The Creator gave us one mouth to feed our body and one mouth to speak the truth. We must learn how to listen first before we speak and we must learn how to tell the truth. When you tell the truth you will have courage and you are respected for your honesty and integrity.

"The Creator gave us only one heart and one mind. Our heart will tell us the right thing to do and our mind will learn all the things we need to know. We must learn how to respect ourselves first, and then we are able to respect others. We must learn to listen to our hearts, and we must learn how to take care of our bodies to live a healthy life.

"The Creator was very smart. He gave us two eyes, two ears, two hands, two feet, one mouth, one mind, and one heart. He gave us a soul and spirit so we can respect our parents and mother earth. The Creator was very smart. We must thank the Creator for giving us these precious gifts."

Shining Gold liked the story and she thanked her grandmother for telling her this story about our precious gifts. She gave her grandmother a great big hug and she went home. The next day Shining Gold felt better and she went back to school. Her grandmother watched her walk to school and Shining Gold walked with her body straight and tall. She had a smile on her face as she thought about the precious gifts she has received from the Creator. Her grandmother knew in her heart that Shining Gold would do well in school.

Shining Gold went to school in the Indian Day School and she was sent to Vancouver to go to high school. This was a cultural shock to her because she lived in a small village all her life. She was not familiar with the big city life. She was fortunate she went to school with her sister, Rose Bell, and her cousin, Sarah Hamilton. They were all living in the same foster house. The first foster parents were nice to them for a while and a month later the foster mother started treating them in a rather cruel manner.

One day they were all sent to the dentist. Shining Gold, Rose, and Sarah did not realize at that time the dentist was making a lot of money by pulling all the native children's teeth. Shining Gold remembers when she was sitting on the dentist chair. She didn't think it was necessary to go to the dentist because she had very good teeth. She remembers the dentist came along and he started pulling all her teeth out. He would pull one teeth out and put it in a little silver bowl. He kept pulling out her teeth and plunking them down, one by one in front of her. Shining Gold's tears were rolling down and she couldn't stop the dentist from pulling all her teeth out. When he started pulling out her "eye teeth," he kept yanking her head back and forth. She cried and cried. There was no one there to help her. Her mother and father did not know the ill treatment she was experiencing. They did not know their daughter was forced to get all her teeth pulled out. When the dentist finished pulling out all Shining Gold's teeth, she walked outside the dentist's office and she fainted on the street.

Shining Gold experienced many difficult times when she was going to school. There were many times she almost gave up, but she remembered the words and advice from her grandmother. She did very well in school and became a teacher. To this day, Shining Gold continues to teach students in Elementary levels and adult classes. She is particularly gifted at teaching literacy and guided reading to students, both within the summer program and with primary level students.

In the year 2000 to 2004, she was a member of the Ministry team. She assisted in revising the curriculum for the B.C. First Nations 11 & 12. She was a representative on the First Nations Education Committee for several years and she was voted as one of the First Nations role model posters. She worked as a First Nations Program Implementer for one year. In this position she had the opportunity to develop and implement a wide range of activities for teachers to improve academic achievement and utilize the First Nations resources. She has experience in developing and delivering education programs and she promoted and worked collaboratively with teachers in implementing First Nations curriculum. She also promoted the Role Model program; it was one of her duties to arrange role models upon teacher requests.

Shining Gold has been teaching primary classes for many years. She is a dedicated teacher and she has the drive and energy to work cooperatively and productively with all the various partners to create a sense of identity and belonging for all students. During her experience as a First Nations Studies 12 teacher, she had the opportunity to develop and maintain relationships with local First Nations community members and she has an intimate knowledge of the First Nations culture and language. Today she is teaching a second generation of children. She is now teaching the children of the students she once taught in grade twelve. No matter where she goes in the community, she always encounters students she taught and she is always eager to greet them and validate their accomplishments.

Sometimes, she encountered a few incidents where she was treated unprofessionally by others, but she always remembers the encouragement and inspiration her grandmother gave her when she was struggling in her early childhood education.

As a teacher her priority is to always make the classroom a safe and welcome environment for all students. She is a strong advocate and team player, and she ensures that she always informs the parents on their child's progress, behaviour, and well-being. When Shining Gold feels sad or encounters difficulties in her professional career, she always remembers the story her grandmother told her about our precious gifts from the Creator.

Eagle Design

My Beautiful Mother

Kaakuns is my dear precious mother, she is my greatest inspiration, my protector, and she is my utmost supporter in my life. She has been there for me in the darkest and most heartbreaking moments in my life. She has comforted me and stood beside me in the happiest times in my life. She always gives me encouragement to reach for the stars and to accomplish my goals in life and education. She is the kindest and most loveable and generous Haida woman I know. She loves and respects me unconditionally, and I love her with all my heart. My mom always said, "Live your life to the fullest when you are young, when you get old, you always think about what you should have done or could have done when you were young. When you get old, your body starts to ache, you can't see very good and you can't walk; that's why I always tell everyone to live their life and do the best you can when you are young." This is my mother's story.

My name is Kaakuns. I was born on August 25, 1927, at Massett, B.C. My parents' names are Amanda Edgars and Isaac Edgars. I have seven children. There names are Isaac White, Pansy Collison, Benjamin White, The Late Herman White, The Late Stolly White, Paul White Jr., and John David White. During those days when I was born there were no nurses or doctors. Mrs. Parnell helped my mom deliver me. I used to wonder why mom used to say Mrs. Parnell was my mother. Even when I grew up, I used to think she was my mother. Then, after I realized that she helped my mother deliver me when I was born. We call her *Kuni,* which means Aunty in the Haida language. I used to stay with Mrs. Parnell when I was a young girl.

The first Haida name I was given was Guulea and then they changed it to Kaakuns. This was my great great grandmother's name. It's a name that has been passed on in our family for generations. My cousin, Rosie Brown, my daughter Pansy, and I have the same name, so that our family names will stay in the *Tsath Lanas* Eagle clan. I have two sisters and three brothers. My sisters' names are Jessie Hamilton and Margaret Hewer. My brothers' names are Jack Edgars, Dean Edgars, and Frank Edgars. My youngest sister's name is Stithkous, which means "One that sits beside the water like St. Mary's springs and we're really proud of you." Mom's grandmother had two Haida names, Guulea and Keet'ta. Mom's name was Wathulcanus. Mom was the matriarch for our family. She has so much knowledge and she knew so many stories. She knew all the people's Haida names, territories, and history. She learned so quick, she didn't even notice it. Her uncles said, "She was born to be like that." Mom was like a walking library. She knew all the songs and she was a great composer of Haida songs.

My family is from the Eagle clan. Our family crests are called: double headed eagle, bear, one finned grey whale, blackfish, forget-me-not flowers, and frog. Each family on Haida Gwaii has their own family names and crests. Our clan name is called *Tsath Lanas.* We call the woman *T'sathjinus.* The *Tsath Lanas* people come from a village called *Jath* located on Langara Island. In the olden days the Islands was called *Gisg'wayah.* Our clan also owns land at Naden Harbour.

Mom used to have the papers for the land, but they were lost at the old band office. I remember when mom used to say, "Don't let anyone walk over us." She meant that she didn't want anyone to take our land while we are all still alive. Mom would be very proud of our clan if she was alive. My daughter did most of the work to get our clan a Chief at Naden Harbour. We had meetings for over one year before we agreed who will be our Hereditary Chief for Naden Harbour. We went by the old traditional Haida way. My brother Dean Edgars is the oldest son of Amanda Edgars, but he didn't want to be our Chief. He said, "My health is not good." So he said he cannot be the Chief. The next one is mom's sister, the Late Minnie Edgars. Ken Edgars was chosen because he was the oldest living son of the Late Minnie Edgars. He was named Chief *Thasi.* I think he is doing really well as our Chief.

We have two lands. *Nonny's* great grandfather was John *Dlawan* from Kung. They thought so much of this place that they took this as their own land in the year 1800. The *Tsath Lanas* people took the best land. Our other Chief's name was Chief *Guulaas.* Our Great uncle's lineage founded this place and they are buried at this place. We own lots of land at Naden Harbour and North Island. Our Chief has to protect our land at Naden Harbour. That's his job as our Hereditary Chief.

This story is about Willie Matthews. Three days before he died, mom went to see him. He was sick in bed and he wanted to see mom. Mom didn't want to go in there without anything, so she bought him a shirt. Even though he has so much family, he was really happy with the shirt. He told mom not to forget about North Island because it is *Tsath Lanas* land. Mom took Willie as an uncle. He gave mom the story. He thought the world of mom because when his mother died, mom's grandmother thought the world of Willie's brother Paul. Paul used to stay with mom's mother (Kate) when his mother died. William Matthews told mom, he said, "Don't ever feel sorry for yourself. Long time ago the *Tsath Lanas* people found the land. The *Tsath Lanas* people are respectable people." During that time, mom was the oldest one from our clan. Now we have to name a Chief for our other land at North Island.

When I was very young about four or five years old, I remember when the Haida people used to row across on their canoes to Alaska. They told me they could walk across Hecate Straits. All around Langara Island, it used to be filled with sea lions. This even happened during our time. Grandfather Guy Edgars used to let us go with him on his rowboat, and we would row as far as the light house. We would stop and scare the sea lions. *Chinny* Guy used to think it was funny, but I used to get a little scared.

He was the only *Chinny* we had and he used to spoil us by taking us out with him, but we learned a lot from him. I remember we used to cry to go out fishing with him. During that time, there were no motors. We just used rowboats and oars. When we went out fishing, we used to stop on the beach and pick *kitons* when the tide was out. When we had enough *kitons, Chinny* Guy would make a big fire on the beach and we would cook the *kitons* right on the beach.

Sometimes, my brothers and sisters would stay up all night until five o'clock in the morning just so we could go out fishing with *Chinny* Guy. We used to get sea pigeons on Langara Island. We call it *Sa'donna* eggs or merits. We would tie a rope around our waists so we could put our hands in the hole to get the eggs. During those days, we used big pots to boil the eggs, but it was hard cleaning the eggs. Everyone used to invite each other. It was like having a big feast. Today, nobody does this anymore. All the eggs are gone.

Chinny Guy used to take us up the Inlet. There was one Island there full of seagulls. We used to go and pick the seagull eggs and pick seaweed. We would go to *Yan* Village, first to pick seaweed and two or three months later we would go to North Island to pick seaweed because the seaweed grows later at North Island. Then we went to get sockeye at *Yan* River. Everybody used to half dry the sockeye and put it in salt. In the winter time we ate the salted down sockeye. It's just like a dream to me, but I remember when *Chinny* Guy used to bury the dog salmon heads in the month of September. The dog salmon heads cooks underneath the ground. *Chinny* Guy left it there for three weeks. Then we would eat it. It tasted so good. I haven't tasted it for years and years. Nobody makes it anymore. When mom used to live at North Island, her grandmother, *Nonny* Guulea had the biggest feast. Mom always talks about this.

There were all kinds of fishermen on rowboats. During that time they did not have gas boats. The year is about 1918. They used canoes and rowboats. *Nonny* Guulea was the first one to have a feast there. What they did is they used flour sacks and they washed all the sacks and hung it out and the sacks got really white. They put all the flour sacks on the grass and they used to say it looked like the grass was already cut from the flour sacks. *Nonny* Guulea invited all the fishermen to the feast. There was a Chief from the mainland and she made Eliza and George Jones sit beside the Chief because she had a lot of respect for these men. When they were getting ready for the feast, she made *Nonny* Hannah and Dora Brook's mother tie up apples and oranges on a tree. Then the fishermen had to pick the apples and oranges off the tree and put them in a basket. *Nonny* Hannah said the oranges were the hardest ones to tie up with string.

Mom had lots of respect for George and Elizah Jones. When she was born, it was George and Eliza Jones who gave Mom her name, Amanda Lucy. They just loved her. They named her Lucy after Lucy Island. Mom's father was part Tlingit. When Mom was nine years old, he tried to take her away from Oceanic cannery. Her father tried to take her away, but her uncle's hid her away. Mom still remembers this.

When I was seven years old, my mother started teaching us Haida songs. We used to learn from Mrs. Brook's mother. Her name was Gootedince and she was the only grandmother we had. I remember when we were very little; she used to tell us stories. We all used to sit around her. It didn't matter where we were, whether we were out camping or at home. We would sit around *Nonny* Gootedince and she would tell us stories. She was really old. Sometimes she would go to sleep and we would still be sitting there waiting for her to wake up so she could tell us stories. Now we don't have anybody to tell us stories.

I remember when there was a potlatch in the Haida community hall. I was about seven years old. I don't know who gave the potlatch, but they made me and my sister Margaret and my brother sing a Haida song. There were visitors from other villages and from the Mainland. We sang one of the Haida songs mom taught us. "*Hi yah slakwiyah nika, nee loo dell son gwon son nika kaw lah, aw lee, aw lah.*"

It's a really sad song. It's a really poor people's song and the way you interpret the song, it is really sad. I don't know who composed this song and I don't know who the song belongs too. We sang this song and our great Uncles John and Phillip and Uncle Frank Bell came up to mom's house the next day. They told mom to teach us better songs because the song we sang means it's a poor people's song. We never sang this song again.

There are lots of songs we used to sing, but I'm forgetting them. But when my sisters Jessie and Margaret sing the songs, I remember them. There is one song about when our grandparents used to chase us to bed. It's called *Yanne-googwah.* Mom and dad used to say, "When you are bad, *Yanne-goodgwah* is going to come and get you." I remember when Jack and I used to fight so much. Mom tied us together when I was seven years old. Mom never forgot it when she tied us together. It's funny now. My sister Jessie was always quiet all the time, even when we were young. Someone made a song out of *Yanne-googwah.* When I was a little girl, I used to imagine *Yanne-googwah* was really big and it had fur all over it like a big animal. I guess that's what they call *Yanne-googwah.*

Mom was a good Haida composer. She made songs most of her life. Mom made songs about my brothers and sisters and she made songs about her grandchildren. When she went to Victoria to perform in the First Nations Olympics, she made up a song about when she went on the airplane. My two daughters, Pansy and Stolly and my two sons, Paul and Johnny were dancing in mom's Haida Eagle dance group during that time. When mom came back from Victoria, she used to say; "I went to university." She said this because the whole dance group was staying at the university quarters.

Mom composed songs for her sister Minnie Edgars. She

composed a song for Jack when he got married to Lena and she also made a song for Caroline Bell's family. She made a song for herself, when she was left alone. She was staying in her new house, when dad died, she had no where to turn. When dad died, Dorothy Fiveland took her to Skidegate. Uncle Solomon Wilson was feeling bad because there were no more old people left. We're all from *Jath*. Solomon Wilson is from *Jath*. Solomon is mom's uncle. Solomon's uncle went to a different land. Solomon's dad picked another land and then some other people started building there. When they came back to *Gisgwhyah,* they took a big boat and they went to another land. His dad found another place to live, that's why people thought so much of Solomon Wilson. Solomon said, "We got to have this place to live at." This is how the *Tsath Lanas* people split up from North Island. Solomon Wilson didn't want mom to forget about this story, so mom could tell this story. When he was telling mom the story, he was really happy because mom knew this story already. North Island is called *Gisgwhyah* and Langara Island. They spread out, going to different places such as Skidegate and Hydaburg. Solomon was telling mom about his only son. John died way before he did. Solomon thought the world of mom because in the Haida way my mom's mother is his sister. We have a big family.

Today our connection is with Aunty Pat, Aunty Stolly, Diane Brown, and Lonnie Young. William Sampson was from *Jath*. This was mom's uncle. Mom and Reggie Sampson were both from *Tsath Lanas* clan. They are just like a brother and sister. They always talked only in the Haida language. William Sampson got married at Port Simpson. William wrote a letter to mom two weeks before he died. Mom feels bad she didn't see him.

When I was young, *Nonny* Gootedince used to tell us about the land. She told us this story: Harry Bell's father is buried at Naden Harbour. His father's name is Peter Bell. That is one of Phillip Bell's brothers. They are mom's real uncles. They buried him there because during that time, they used to think a lot of their land. They had respect for the land and nobody was allowed to build around their grave. They just kept the land for themselves. The other headstone is on Langara Island. The little point where the headstone is called *Dadens*. During those days, *Dadens* was only a little point. We used to live there and Dora Brook's mom used to show us where the headstones are located. At that time everyone used to live in big houses. There used to be a fire right in the middle of the house. I still remember this and I still talk about *Dadens* because I heard the story from my grandmother when I was a little girl.

I remember when we were quite young, we used to go up the Inlet on a rowboat and we used to have two sets of oars and sometimes there were four boats that went up together. No men, all women and children. We went up the Inlet on the rowboats to camp. All the men were out fishing. I used to like going out with mom and the other Haida women. We used to stop and go camping wherever the river was running and put up our tents. Sometimes we used to stay in some of the houses along the way up to the Inlet.

Nonny Kildoway was my grandfather's sister. She used to have her own rowboat and mom had her own rowboat too. All the women used to go up the Inlet and we would pick all kinds of berries. We used to pick berries for everyone. We used to jar it and our boat was filled with canned berries. We even killed one seal, the only one we got. Mom fried baking powder biscuits from the oil. After we picked the berries, we canned all the berries and left it up the Inlet because it was too heavy to take down on the rowboats. People never used to take it. The berries were always there when we went back up the Inlet to get the berries. I really miss that because today nobody goes out on rowboats anymore.

Everybody used to be healthy during that time. I guess because they are out in the fresh air and eating fresh food. I didn't start school until I was nine years old because mom and dad used to take us to different places and camps to gather food. Every four months we would move to different places and go work at different canneries. In the camps, dad used to go fishing for crabs and he would sell it and mom would preserve the rest for winter time. After the canneries closed down at Naden Harbour, we used to move to North Island and then dad would start trolling.

I remember when I was twelve years old, the cannery closed down at Naden. We all moved over to Shannon Bay and then the cannery closed there. Then we went to Ian River. That is where we got the salmon and sockeye. Lots of people used to live there. They used to smoke, dry and can all the salmon and deer meat. Then we went out to dig clams. Mom used to dry and smoke the clams and put them all around the stove. They used big sticks and dad used to get a thick wire and hang the clams so it could dry and smoke around the fire. They used to salt down the salmon so everything will be ready for winter. That was the last thing they did at the end of the year.

Dad and all the Haida men never used to work on Sunday. We used to look forward to Sunday because dad used to take us out for a picnic on his big boat. He never used to go fishing on Sunday. All his brothers, Timothy, Joe, and Jimmy Edgars were like that. The whole family would spend some time together and have an enjoyable day. I remember when I used to go fishing with dad all the time and we used to go out fishing with *Chinny* Guy. He was the only grandfather I had. I didn't know mom's father and I didn't know mom's mother because her mom (Kate Guulea Bell) died when she was only nine years old. That's why her Uncle Phillip, Uncle John, Uncle Peter, and Uncle Frank raised her.

During that time we just used to row out in the Inlet to go fishing. *Chinny* Guy used to take only two of us at the time because he had so many grandchildren. Dolly Parnell and I went out with *Chinny* Guy and we used to row while he sat at the back of the rowboat with his fishing gear. It was lots of fun. When we came home everyone used to run down to the beach and meet us when we came home from fishing. All the grandchildren used to push the rowboat out and anchor it out in the water. We used to fight over who was going to pull in the anchor. Dad used to anchor his boat out so no one will play on the boat and fall in the water. Then *Chinny* Guy used to go sell the salmon and buy us apples, oranges, and candy. He was really kind and he spoiled all his grandchildren.

When I started school, I didn't even know how to speak English. During that time everyone was sent away to residential school. But dad never let any of his kids go to residential school. That's why mom and dad used to take us all over the Islands, when the Indian Agent came to take away the kids. The government used to send all the kids away. I remember when they sent Zola and Nina Williams out to school. Their dad had a great big seine boat called the Adelaide Jay. That was George Jones's boat. During that time everyone used to have seine boats. The boat called Western Hope came and took a lot of the kids away to residential school. They put them on the boat and send them to Alert Bay and *Coqualeetza*. They just used to send the kids out. That's the government's work, but mom and dad wouldn't let them take any of us. Dad said, he's going to look after his own kids and feed them himself. I remember, I used to want to go, but dad would not send us away to residential school. I think that is why we know a lot of our Haida stories and a lot of our culture.

Most of the older kids were sent out to residential school: Aunty Dorothy Bell, Aunty Ethel Jones, and Aunty Bessie Widen. They stayed there for many years. My husband, Paul White Sr. had to go when he was really young. He had to stay there because his parents couldn't pay his fare back for holidays. Lots of them used to stay down there and they never used to come home. My husband stayed there for about seven years. He hardly stayed with his mom and dad. But he wouldn't send any of our children to residential school.

He did the same thing as my mom and dad and he wouldn't allow the Indian Agent to take our children to residential school. He experienced part of his life at these schools, so he didn't want his own children to be sent away to residential school. I started school when I was nine years old. I wasn't good at speaking English. I was always willing to do anything. I helped the teachers after school and they started making me work as a janitor. I was nine years old. I worked there until I was fifteen years old. I used to try really hard to get my work done early so I could ring the bell after school. I used to pack three foot long wood in to the school so there was enough wood to burn in the stove for one day. Mom and dad used to come down to help me sometimes. I had to scrub three classrooms on my hands and knees. It was a lot of work and I was there all by myself. The teachers didn't leave until I finished all the work. I was getting five dollars a month for all that work. During those days, they used to ration food for five dollars for each person.

I was quite young. I started thinking I could make more money working at the old cannery, so I started working there. I was fifteen years old when I quit school. I went to the Indian Day School in Old Massett village. Miss Curry was my teacher and then when I was in grade five my teacher's name was Miss Kennedy. When I quit school, I started working for Clarence Martin. He got married to my teacher, Miss Kennedy. They were my only two teachers in school. Later, I started working for Mr. Martin's mother. She had a great big store right by the New Massett dock. They had a great big house. It was two stories high. I remember when it burned down. They were really rich people.

I started working in the school and then in the cannery. The first thing I bought myself was a bed and drawers. I started working for Mr. Martin when I was fifteen years old and then I worked for Mr. Lindner for almost five years. I was working and cleaning up their hotel. Kurt Lindner's wife owned the hotel and Kurt owned the store. I hardly stayed home because I worked all over. I can't believe that I worked all my life.

I'm eighty years old and I will be eighty one years old on August 25, 2008 and I'm still working and teaching the Haida language. I started working when I was nine years old and I made my daughter Pansy start working when she was twelve years old. She started working at the cannery at New Massett. She worked really hard for five years and then she finally received her first pay cheque when she was sixteen years old. She came down to work in the cannery every day after school. Many times we had to work until midnight.

During those days we worked by "piece work" and not by the hour. We worked really hard cracking and shaking all the crabs all day and night. When Pansy came to work after school, she was in grade six. I can't believe I made her work so hard. I would shake all the meat out of the crabs and the claws was piled high over my head. When my daughter came to work after school, she worked really fast. All the other ladies would give us their small claws. We made more money by the pounds because we both worked fast and they paid us more money for the small claws.

Sometimes we worked past midnight and my daughter had to go to school the next day. She worked in the cannery until she was seventeen years old. Then the manager sent the fastest workers to Port Edward cannery. Pansy, Eleanor Russ, Caroline Bell, and her sisters were really fast workers. The manager sent them to Port Edward cannery to work. The Bell sisters are still working in the cannery today. They are all good workers and they are all quiet kind girls. Today, they don't work by piece work. They are paid by the hour. When you get paid by the hour, it isn't as good as working by piece work for crabs.

When I ran away from home, I was fifteen years old and I went to work in the cannery at Hydaburg, Alaska. They wouldn't let me work because I didn't have any ID so I stayed with Uncle Pete. He thought the world of mom and he was really happy when I could talk Haida to him. Uncle Pete said, "Don't get married outside of Massett." He said, "It's too hard, look I'm really lonely. I have no relatives here besides my own kids." I never forgot his advice. Uncle Pete had three seine boats, so he took me to Rose Inlet to see if I could get a job in the cannery, but they said I was too young. I stayed there for one week, then I went back home to Massett. I worked all the time in different canneries. Then later after many years, my feet started to swell up. I was using boots and my feet used to swell up really big. I used to have real hard time taking off my boots. That's the time when my daughter was working there too and the nurse got me a job in a dry place. That's why I'm like this now, my body hurts and pains with arthritis. I worked too hard in the cannery. My feet started swelling up, and I showed it to the doctor down the village.

I couldn't take my boots off. The doctor had to cut my boots off. He said I had arthritis; I had to quit working in the cannery. They got me to work in the school. They said I was getting rheumatism. I was so crazy, I never stop working. I've been working in both schools for over thirty years. After I worked in the cannery, I started working in the school. First I started working at George M. Dawson High School and then they moved me down to *Tahayghen* Elementary School. The school wasn't open yet, but I had to go there and scrub all the floors. Ted Sheppard was the boss and I remember I had a tough time using the polisher. Eventually, I got used to using the big polisher. No one was around, but I used to have a hard time.

After I worked there for over twenty years, I got used to working with the polisher. I think that's why I was well known up New Massett. I worked everywhere and I worked at so many places. I have been teaching the Haida language for many years. When the new Chief Matthews School opened, the band council hired Margaret and I. We were teaching daily words, greetings, things that grow, months and when berries grow. We taught about what grows in each season. In the spring, summer, fall, and winter time. We also taught the students how they are related to each other and what clan they belong too. Margaret made the students line up and she called out the name of each clan. The students would go to their clan. It was really cute. The kids were six years old. They were so small and they were really happy when they went to their clan. It was just like they were meeting each other for the first time. They all sat together in their clan.

The kids were happy to sit down beside each other. Then they said who they are related too. Margaret was really good at telling them what they should call each other. We taught the kids a lot of Haida words. They were easy to talk too and they listened and learned really fast. I liked it when Margaret used to play the drum and sing Haida songs to the kids. I really liked to teach the language. We'd go to Sibby's house every Saturday. Candy and Sibby took all the food. We used to take some food and they told us not to take the food anymore. There was Ethel Jones, Mary Swanson, Nina Williams, Steven Brown, and I. We would teach the young mothers who are interested in learning the Haida language.

When it was my turn to speak Haida, I tell them what they are cooking in the Haida language. They really enjoyed learning. I like to teach the language and I will teach it as long as I can. I do the best I can when I am teaching the language. I enjoy teaching all the children. I'm willing to teach them anything they need to know, so they will be proud of who they are. Then they can teach the other children the Haida language and culture.

I retired from the school in 1972. Four months after I retired, I went to Hawaii. Aunty Goose, John Chutter, Allan Wilson, Annabel, and Grace Wilson were going to Hawaii one week after I retired. They asked me to go and I went with them. We stayed in Hawaii for one month. It was really nice down there. While I was there, I felt really good. There was nothing wrong with me. I had no aches or pains. It's like I was pretending to be sick when I went back home. I think it was the good weather and good people. Then when I went back home, I started to get sick again. I really enjoyed it at Hawaii. I didn't want to go back home. Since my retirement, I have been travelling all over the world.

I always wanted to go to New Zealand. Margaret and I

started teaching the Haida language at Chief Matthews School and we were chosen to go to New Zealand. Things always turn out good for me. When we were going to New Zealand, Margaret knew I couldn't push her on the wheelchair, so they chose Aunty Dorothy Bell to go and Ernie Collison. I always want to talk about this trip, but nobody cares to listen. When we were in New Zealand, we went to every house. They start teaching the little children all the same age in one house. Their uncles or sisters or family take the children. We went to see the older children at another house. It's just like a school. They are just like us. They eat food from the beach and all the seafood we eat.

They cooked us scrambled eggs everyday and they let us eat all the time. They were always taking good care of us. It was a big place. The kids had to be the same height. Some are tall, but they are still young. All the kids learn how to talk their language. Every post has a totem pole, even in front of the house and the fences are carved. There were carvings all over. They are doing well because they all work together. There is a place where they all carve. All the posts are all carved all around the inside of the big building. They are like longhouses, but there are no beds in there. There is also a place for computers and everyone has to learn their language before they start school. Everyone gets up and gives a speech in their language.

I did a lot of travelling and then my son, Super encouraged me to go to the repatriation committee meetings. They were just starting and I was interested as an Elder. Sometimes these young people need advice, so I went to all the meetings. Lucille Bell was one of the first ones to start this group. I enjoy going to the repatriation meetings. We were the first ones that started going to these meetings. They picked me for one of the committees. I helped out when they were fundraising for our travel costs. We had to raise a lot of money.

Chief *Thasi*, Ken Edgars and his wife Barb Edgars, Mary Swanson, Vince Collison, Leona Clow, and I always go to all the meetings. The first place we went to was Victoria, B.C. I don't know how many years we were in the committee before they sent the first group of people down to Victoria. Vince Collison, Mary Swanson, Lucille Bell, Ken Edgars, Barb Edgars, Reno Russ, and I. Only a few of us went to Victoria. This was our first trip. Mary and I were the witnesses, when the men were wrapping up the remains. It was really sad for me. There were a lot of Haida dancers from Seattle and Vancouver. We had places to stay and everyone treated us really good. After that we went to New York and Chicago. I don't know if they will pick me again, but I want to go to Washington on the next trip. I'm really proud of Lucille Bell for all the work she does with the repatriation group. I think all our ancestors are smiling down on all the people that helped bring them back home to Haida Gwaii.

When I was a teenager, I remember nobody was allowed to go out after nine o'clock. George Price used to come out on the road and blow his bugle at nine and everybody had to go home. The Haida people used to be really strict. They used to look after their kids really good. I remember when they picked Paul (my future husband) to be a constable. He used to send all the kids home. I remember when we saw him coming down the road, we used to run away from him and hide under houses. (Kaakuns laughs really hard as she remembers when they used to run away from Paul White Sr.) Nina and Zola Williams, Betty Thompson, Adelia, and Alberta; we all used to run away from him and call him all kinds of names. Paul used to tell this story to his kids.

"Your mom used to be really bad. When I was a constable, she used to run away from me and I couldn't catch her. By golly, I caught her in the end and I married her." When my mom got married, she had an arranged marriage. Her uncles arranged her marriage. They picked Isaac Edgars for mom and they got married. Mom used to laugh really hard when she tells us about her marriage. She said she didn't want to lay down with him. But they had a good marriage and dad was the kindest man in the world. He loved all of us and they were our teachers.

They taught us how to fish, hunt, gather, and preserve

food. They taught us the Haida stories and culture. I also learned how to knit and crochet. I knitted all my children their own clothes and socks. I never had to buy any clothes because I sewed and knitted all their clothes. Lots of Haida women did their own sewing. Even my mom used to make our own petty coats, pants, and dresses.

My marriage was not an arranged marriage. I got married when I was twenty-one years old and Paul was twenty-eight years old. My mother in law, Elizah lost her eye sight before we got married. She couldn't see my oldest son, Isaac when he was born. I remember she had bad eyes and she couldn't sleep. She used to stay up all night because her eyes used to hurt too much. It could have being saved because she could see a little light, but she couldn't see a doctor during that time. Her son, Douglas White had to go to Miller Bay hospital, so my oldest son, Isaac (also called by his nickname, Super) went to stay with my mother-in-law. My kids called her Big *Nonny* but her name was Elizah White. They called her Big *Nonny* and they called my mom Small *Nonny*. I guess because the difference in their size so they wouldn't get mixed up with which grandmother they are talking about. My son, Super was five years old when he started staying with Big *Nonny*. She never used to sleep in. She would get up early in the morning to cook for Super. In the winter time we used to flash down to their house to see if they were awake. Super used to flash back to us. This was our way of checking to see if they were alright.

My son stayed with his grandmother until he was twelve years old. When I first got married, Paul and I used to look after a lot of kids. I don't know why we did this. They used to like to stay with us. Vivian Davis, Ruby Brown, Lena Edgars, and Joyce Williams. I remember when Joyce went to Port Edward to stay with her Aunty. She didn't come back. She died. I always felt bad about this. Her mother's name was Pansy Williams. I named my oldest daughter after her. Ruby stayed with us the longest and she used to love to take care of my daughter. She changed her about three or four times a day and she was always bathing her. Alice Jones was Ruby's mom and she is my husband's first cousin. Alice Jones was Agnes William's oldest daughter and when she passed away, the kids started staying with us.

I remember I looked after my dad when he had a stroke, I was back and forth, same thing with mom and I'm glad I did this. I looked after both of them. I always had two houses to look after, from the time I remember. I used to go back and forth from our house to my parent's house. I used to go out to get wood on my little truck at *Tow* Hill, while they were building our house. I used to go out during the weekend, but dad made me quit because I was by myself and he started coming out with me.

I filled the truck up with wood that has a lot of bark because they burn longer, so I picked this kind of wood. This was just lately when dad was alive. I was in the hospital when dad died. Then I got out of the hospital. I knew he was going to die. The doctor told me he had a heart attack. The third time was really bad. He got a stroke and he couldn't walk and he didn't even get sick all his life. The doctor's couldn't find any records on him. He didn't get sick, so there weren't any records, but when he got older his heart bothered him.

I used to go out to get seaweed on a small boat. When I got married, I used to go out all by myself and sometimes with my cousins. One time I went to *Yan* Village by myself. I used a little dingy and rowed across to *Yan* Village to pick seaweed. Wilfred Marks went on his own boat and I was rowing just behind them. They were watching me and then they couldn't find me. After I picked seaweed, they towed me behind their big boat. Wilfred said, "Don't go out by yourself again; your skiff is too small. Your husband has a big boat."

I remember another time when Laura, Alberta, and I went out picking seaweed. We got ten sacks of seaweed all by ourselves. The rocks were just thick with seaweed. The Haida people call this black gold and when they dry it all up, they call it Indian popcorn. It's funny; Alberta White, Laura Parnell and I still talk about it today. We got stuck in a tide rip and we were really scared. (Kaakuns laughs really hard) I wonder how we dried it. I remember now my mom and dad dried the seaweed.

We used to go hunting by ourselves on mom's rowboat when we were teenagers. One time June Russ and I went out hunting and Mom came with us. We went rowing up the Inlet. I saw one deer, I aimed at the deer, but I couldn't shoot it. So I started running after the deer, but the deer was too fast for me. Even women used to go hunting.

I remember when Uncle Phillip Bell went without eating for forty days. He walked around the house feeling really bad. He made my mom go up the Inlet to get all her salmon in the month of September. He didn't want mom to know he was going to pass away. He knew he was going to die and he wanted to come up to my house. During that time when the Haida people knew they were going to die, they used to stay with someone else, someone like their aunty, uncle, or relative. He could have been the last one that did this in the old traditional way. When Alice Gold was really sick, she wanted to go to Lena and Joe Edgar's house. She made her husband take her to their house. I always think about this, because I think that is where mom and dad went that night.

My brother, Jack, and I were going to bed. We used to have a big hallway and a big porch. Our bedrooms were up stairs and we used to have an outside house at the back of our house. We were going outside and I wanted to use the bathroom. I opened the door and Jack was right behind me. He was really small and we saw something really white by the door. It was really white. Two of us saw this. It was really calm, no wind. I'll never forget this because I was screaming really hard. The older people said if you see something that really scares you, and then you put something in your mouth, even if it's a big nail or something solid. I was holding the flashlight and I put the flashlight in my mouth. I'm really old fashion. I believe it when the older people tell me something about our traditions and culture.

In the olden days when we were kids, we used to cover the

mirrors and no one in the village was allowed to turn on the radio when some one died. Everyone in the village had to be really quiet and have respect for the loved one that died. Every one paid respect for the loved one that passed away. Even today there are some people that still do this. Some people cover the mirrors and television. That is how much they have respect for the person that passed away. If a person from the Eagle clan died, it is the tradition of the Haida people that the Raven clan members stay up all night to guard and protect the body of the deceased person. The Raven clan also digs the grave and when it is time to move a headstone, it is the Raven clan that wipes the headstone. When the Eagle clan puts on a potlatch, they pay the Raven clan members that helped out. They write down their names and they are paid at the potlatch and acknowledged for all the kind work they did for the Eagle clan.

When my mom was alive, my oldest sister, Jessie, and I took Mom up to Alaska. We took her to see *Nonny* Sli. *Nonny* Sli was 106 years old and she was married to Mom's uncle. She was really small and we used to have lots of fun. We took mom over to visit *Nonny* Sli one week after her birthday. She was really old, but she didn't look old. She looked just as old as mom. Mom was eighty-two years old and *Nonny* Sli was 106 years old. At that time *Nonny* Sli was feeling really sick. Her daughter was a nurse, so Louise stayed home with her mom.

When we arrived, her mom used to just stay in bed and she wouldn't eat. When she heard Mom was here, she got up and sat up all afternoon with Mom. They were singing Haida songs all afternoon. Louise could sing the songs too. They were all really happy. They prayed first and then they started singing Haida songs and all the Christian songs in Haida. They talked about all the things they used to do long time ago. They were so cute.

I remember how happy they were. They were singing all the Haida songs. Louise said, "It's like a miracle." Mom said, "It's like a Haida medicine. When you are lonely then when you have someone to talk to in your own language, it's a medicine."

I never forgot this because *Nonny* Sli was really sick and she got better because she was so happy to see Mom.

Today everything is so different. Everything is changing. All our people are spread out all over the country and we're forgetting about each other. I got a big family, but some of them don't call me. I was telling some of my relatives to call me for a cup of coffee. Today, people don't mix up anymore like we used to in the old days. We used to visit each other, help each other, and share a lot of our Haida food. Today, everyone works for themselves and they don't have time to visit each other. Some of my family get me deer meat or sockeye, but most of the time I have to pay for it.

I have a big family. Lucky our own family talks to each other. Rosie Brown and I talk about things we used to do long ago. We talk for hours and hours and she remembers everything Mom and *Nonny* Hannah said to us. I like to visit Nora Samuels. She's got a kind heart and she doesn't say a mean word about anyone. She's a hard working lady, just like me. I remember how Mom loved Rita White so much. She said they are just like sisters, now they are both gone. I think that's how Rosie, Nora, and I feel about each other.

I remember when Clement White got married to Sarah. Clement White is my husband's brother. Mom's uncles had so much respect for Clement, they packed him up from the canoe. They called him *Eeahuk-la-gah.* This is a really big word in the Haida language. Mom's uncle was a Chief. He was married to Awee Yetgah. Her uncle adopted Susan (Nina William's mother) because *Nonny* Yetgah didn't have any kids, so they adopted her. Harry and Henry Geddes were brothers and their mother was Emma White. Emma is Henry White's sister. Henry White is Rufus White's father. Emma White was Connie White's grandmother. Connie White was married to my husband's brother, Douglas White. Connie has two brothers living.

I met one of her brothers and he was really happy to meet me. I'm his Aunty. Henry White was Connie White's uncle. Her mother was Helen Charles. She raised her kids and she had them registered as a Dix. Elsie White got married to a Dix. My husband had a sister named May White. She got married to Bahjoo Parnell. Paul White Sr. had two sisters and one brother. His sister's names were May and Winnie White. His brother's name was Douglas White. Bahjoo, Earl, and Buddy used to call Mom their sister. Pearl Parnell and Mom got along really well. Buddy used to call my Mom his sister.

Sometimes my health gets really bad. Last year I over did it when I drank too much devil's club. I was really sick and I couldn't pull the blankets over myself. One morning I didn't even eat. I drank a really big mouth full of devil's club and I didn't even measure it. Then in the afternoon the medicine started working on me. I started vomiting really hard and I couldn't stop.

My son, Isaac came down to see me and he could see that I couldn't stop vomiting. He got really worried and he wanted to take me to the hospital. I know that I got really sick and I cured myself. I know I am suppose to take a little bit, but I was having a hard time. I ended up curing myself when I was so sick. One time I dreamed about Jessie when I got really sick. In my dream, she was standing beside the bed. She didn't say anything to me. I remember when Jessie got really sick. She phoned me and the same night she passed away. I was thinking about Jessie because my chest is really sore. Jessie talked to me in the Haida language and she told me that her chest was really sore. That same night she got a heart attack and she passed away.

The same thing happened to Mom. I was working at the school. I phoned Jessie to take mom to the hospital. Mom got a heart attack on the taxi. I think she got a heart attack from feeling too bad. Dad used to say, if you know your heart is hurting, just lay still on your back and don't think of anything and it will gradually go away. That's what I've been doing, but I forgot I fell down in the bathroom. That's when I thought it was my heart that was bothering me. That's why I started thinking that I should go to the Prince Rupert hospital. Lucky my daughter in law, Mary Ethel White was with me.

Everything turns out really good for me, because I always ask God to help me. Mary took me to the emergency entrance and the doctor came to see me right away. He asked me if I fell and I forgot about when I fell early in the morning. I didn't get hurt, but I forgot about that. Then Mary reminded me and told the doctor. I couldn't breath right that morning and I thought it was arthritis, but the doctor took x-rays and found out that I had a broken rib.

My health bothers me sometimes, but I'm happy I have my two brother's Dean and Frank Edgars to turn too. I really miss my two sisters, Margaret Hewer and Jessie Hamilton. But I'm glad I have a big family and I can turn to them for help. My mom was right. She said, "When you turn fifty or older, then you will remember all the things we taught you and you will understand what we are saying." Lots of things are coming back to me and I know my mom was right. I am remembering lots of things what mom told me. Mom used to always say, "When you are older, you're going to start thinking about things and what is going to happen." Today, I understand because I have experienced life.

As a parent, when we tell our kids not to do something, they go ahead and do it anyway and they end up learning the hard way. I guess everybody learns about life in different ways. One thing I always remember is when mom told me I was always kind to everybody. She said, "Gertie, everybody doesn't feel the same way you feel towards yourself." There is some nice people and some bad people. Mom said, "If anybody says anything to you or doesn't like you, don't say anything back to them." Mom was right.

Its better not to answer anyone back when someone doesn't like what your family is doing. I remember sometimes when someone says something to hurt my feelings; I hold my tongue and don't say anything. I'm glad I took my mom's advice and now I give the same advice to my children.

One thing I always remember is when *Nonny* Hannah

came to me after my youngest daughter, Stolly died. She always used to come and visit me and tell me stories. She reminded me of Dora Brook's mom. *Nonny* Hannah always called me *Gaadaa*, which means "loved one" or "dear one." She said the *Tsath Lanas* people not suppose to talk about what they do, other people will talk about it and see how they are doing. She said in the Haida language, "I'm really proud of you. People from outside can see what you are doing. You have a big house and you always put on dinners."

What she said really pushed me ahead. Now I can see the way people look at me. I don't tell anybody what I do. People can see what I do. I will always remember what *Nonny* Hannah said to me. I tell my children the same thing. *Nonny* Hannah, Dora Brooks, Rita White, and Leila Abrahams are all my family. We all belong to the *Tsath Lanaas* clan. *Nonny* Hannah's brothers are Amos Williams and John Williams. They are our uncles. We have lots of relatives at Skidegate. The Late Connie Morris was the one that kept us together. She was really kind and she treated us really good. Now her sisters, Stolly and Pat are taking over to keep our families together. Stolly, Pat, Ada, and Aunty Connie have lots of good children that will carry on and keep our families together. We have lots of family in Hydaburg. Mary Morris is really close to us. She is our family. We have lots of family; we just have to tell all our kids and grandchildren so they all get to know each other.

The hardest thing I went through is when we lost five in our family in four years. I made my oldest daughter, Pansy May work really hard in the cannery when she was twelve years old. My daughter and I worked so we could buy the headstones for my youngest daughter Stolly, my son Herman, and my husband Paul White Sr. Only two of us made enough money from working in the cannery to buy the headstones. Some people used to think I was happy, but I used to cry all the time. I missed my children that died and my husband. My husband drowned and mom said the Haida believe that when a person drowns they turn into a killer whale.

One day, I remember when it was really calm weather. There were a lot of people in front of our house looking out in the water. There were three killer whales right in front of our house. The killer whales stopped and were swimming in a circle. They swam in a circle four times and started swimming past our house. I always think about this. My son Herman and my daughter, Stolly both died suddenly. They were both healthy and strong young teenagers.

My husband was alive then and he told all of us to take all our clothes we were wearing and burn them. It wasn't easy for me, now I look back. We had a memorial potlatch for my family that passed away. When we gave the potlatch, it seemed like a big burden was lifted from my shoulders. We thanked all the people who helped us when I lost my children and my husband. My son, Paul White Jr. designed a special Haida print to give to everyone to thank them for coming to the potlatch. My oldest daughter wrote a poem for her sister, brother, and dad. My son's Paul, Benny, and Johnny all danced with the Haida Eagle dancers and they sang songs and danced at the potlatch.

I'm really proud of all my kids, they are all doing well. Altogether, I had seven kids, but after I lost one son and one daughter. I really love my children and try my best to help them out in anything they need to succeed in life. I have twenty grandchildren, twelve great grandchildren, and two great-great grandchildren.

My son, Paul White Jr. is an excellent carver and artist. He carved mom's memorial totem pole that was raised and put beside my house in the Village. He carves out of gold, silver, and cedar wood. He is an excellent artist. He makes all the designs for my button blankets and vests. He carves beautiful rings and bracelets out of silver and gold. My son has a kind heart. People can see how he treats other people and they say he is a kind man. He's teaching my grandsons how to carve. I'm really happy to see how my grandsons, John, Paul, and Fraser are learning how to carve from my son. They are both doing really good carving in silver and gold.

My daughter, Pansy is a hard worker and a good teacher. She does everything. She is a weaver. She makes drums, button blankets, vests, and regalia. She is good at politics and she has a strong voice when she speaks in public gatherings. She does everything for our family. She uses her education well and she does all the writing and paperwork for most of our clan.

My son, Isaac is a good logger. He worked most of his life at logging camps. Then he started getting sick after he worked as a welder for many years. I'm happy he really listened to my dad about carving paddles. He makes really good paddles. Today, he works hard at whatever he does and I'm proud of him.

My son, Ben has worked for Rivtow for over thirty years. He is just like his *Nonny* Elizah. He always keeps his house really clean. He is also a baker and cook, but he works at Rivtow Ltd. He knows the whole North Coast area. I'm proud of him because when the electric equipment doesn't work, I know my son can guide the boat back. He knows how to tell the land really good and he can navigate the boat without using the new modern equipment. You take away all the equipment and he can navigate any boat back to land safely.

My son, Johnny works at the cannery and he works as a clam digger. He gets me all the seafood I need and he takes good care of me all the time. All my children are doing good. I don't have to worry about them, but as a mother I guess I'll always worry.

I have lots of grandchildren. I remember when I was really sick, my granddaughter, Pansy Snow White always came to help me out at my house. Before that she used to live with me. She always helped me out with everything. One time when I was sick, she put the blankets on me to cover me up. Then she said to me, "What else do you want, Queen." She made me laugh really hard.

All my grandchildren are doing well. I always tell them, I didn't go to school that's why I'm always sick. I worked too hard. I always encourage my grandchildren to keep going to school. They must get an education to get a job today. I'm really proud of all my grandchildren. You never notice my granddaughter, Stolly. She is studying, but she is really smart. Some ways she is on the quiet side. She doesn't talk fast and I'm proud she is doing very well in college and she has her diploma in Culinary Arts.

My grandchildren are always there to help me. When I was going to Prince Rupert, my granddaughter Sharleen White said, "*Nonny* you should take dad with you. I think if he goes out and has a rest, he will get better." Sharleen thinks about everybody. My son always sends his children down to my house to help me. His twin daughters are now going to College at Terrace B.C. to get their Early Childhood Education certificate. I think they will both do really good because they love to work with children. I'm really proud of Kathleen and Darleen; I know they will do good.

I had a good life. I have my children that I love and I was blessed with many grandchildren and great grandchildren. I have travelled all over the world and I've seen many different places. Now I'm living for my family. I give them support and encouragement all the time. They can always come to me for advice. As long as I live, I will help out all my children and grandchildren.

I will always give advice and support Ken Edgars. He is our Hereditary Chief. We all have to work to support one another, so we can get ahead. We have to be proud of who we are. It's very important that we treat everyone in our clan with respect. There are so many people in our clan. We have to get along and work together. We have to get to know each other and help each other. My most important wish is to know that my daughter and sons will always love each other and take care of each other. I want all my grandchildren and great grandchildren to love their parents and treat them with respect.

I will always be here for all my nephews and nieces. I like it when they come to visit me. I like to cook for them. I tell them to help themselves when they come to visit me. They make me happy. I love all my brothers' and sisters' kids. I love all my grandchildren and our whole family.

I want to leave this story as part of my legacy of my life for all my family and clan. I hope they all have a good life and learn our language and culture. I'm willing to teach them anything they need to know, so that they will be proud of who they are and teach their children our culture. I have worked hard all my life and now I'm getting old. I can feel my body hurts and it's getting harder for me to get around, but I have lived a good life.

I'm happy with what I accomplished in my life. Now I will live for my children and family. When it is time for me to go see my husband and family in the spirit world, I'll be happy to see them because I lived a good life and I have worked hard on this earth. This story is a gift for all my children, grandchildren, and family. I love all of them with all my heart.

Tribute to My Mother

In loving memory of my mother, Gertie White, born August 25, 1927.

On October 11, 2007, my mother travelled to the land of souls. During her life she worked hard and she set the bar high as a hard working Haida lady. Mom started working when she was nine years old. She worked as a janitor for the Old Massett Day School for several years. During those days she packed enough wood to keep the stove burning all day. She scrubbed the floors and cleaned three classrooms for $5.00 a month. When she was fifteen years old she started working in the cannery. She worked in several canneries at Masset, Port Edward, and in Alaska for many years. Then she worked as a custodian for over thirty years in all three schools in New Massett. After she retired from working in the schools, she enjoyed travelling to Hawaii, Hydaburg, Alaska, Vancouver, Victoria, and New Zealand. Her retirement didn't last long. She became a Haida teacher at Chief Matthews School and both high schools. During the last few years of her life, she taught the Haida language to all the young children and young adults. She enjoyed teaching all the children their language and culture. My mother was a very independent and dedicated worker. She worked until she was a graceful age of eighty years old.

During her life she was always eager and concerned about the politics of the Haida Nation. She always attended the local Band Council public meetings and Council of Haida Nation meetings. She loved to go to church to listen to Reverend Lily Bell preach the word of God, and she was a dedicated member of the Repatriation Committee. She always said, "Our ancestors are really proud of all the Haida people who came to take the remains of our ancestors' home to Haida Gwaii. Now they are resting in peace." She travelled to New York, Chicago, Washington, Victoria, and Vancouver with the Repatriation Group members.

Mom loved to go to the All Native Tournament in Prince Rupert to cheer on the Haida boys. She was always so proud of all the Haida men from Massett, Skidegate, and Hydaburg, Alaska. She enjoyed going to the Civic Center to eat all the delicious native food, talk to people, and cheer on all the Haida teams. She loved to play bingo and she enjoyed going out to celebrate the victory, when the Haida teams won the championship.

She loved to sing Haida songs and she was always so proud of all her children for carrying on the Haida traditions. Mom was rather shy when she first started dancing, then she became more confident and she loved to perform and sing Haida songs. She was truly proud of all her grandchildren and great grandchildren. Mom was an honorable, elegant Haida woman. She was grateful when the Haida people gave her seafood, clams, deer meat, or sockeye. When she received any kind of seafood, she would say, "I don't know if I should salt it, dry it, smoke it, or can it." She always got so excited when anyone gave her deer meat or seafood. She was a kind, caring, and giving person who continuously encouraged all her grandchildren to get an education and, most of all, to respect their mother and father. Every one of us will always have our own special memories of Mom.

Memories by Miranda Young

The last few days being with *Nonny* were one of the hardest things. Thinking of you when you were once so healthy and strong. I can still picture you pushing your cleaning supplies down the hall at George M. Dawson High School, when I was going to school.

G is for the GREAT life we have had because of our *Nonny* Gertie.

E is for the EVERLASTING tears we will have in losing you.

R is for the beautiful ROSES that await you at the Golden Gates.

T is for the TENDER loving care that you showed to everyone.

I is for the INSPIRATION that you gave to everyone you encountered in your life.

E is for EVERLASTING love and precious memories we will always cherish.

You are resting peacefully now *Nonny*, and I know that everyone that has gone before you is standing there with open arms of love. Would you please give them a hug and kiss for me to let them know that I love them too. Till we meet again *Nonny*, I will always love and miss you.

Memories by Pansy Snow White

I was always *Nonny* Gertie's precious "baby" ever since I was a young girl. I always went on trips with her. She would tell me before we would go to the mall that I could buy one thing, but I always wanted more and she would get it for me. She taught me how to drive a car and after that I always wanted to go to the beach at *Tow* Hill and drive her car. There is so much I can say about her, but I will always keep my own special memories of my *Nonny*. I love her so much and I will miss her.

Memories by Erica Collison

When I was young, I heard the older people call her "Aunty Gertie," so I grew up calling her Aunty; it was just my way of calling her *Nonny*. She once said, "You make me feel so young when you call me Aunty." Aunty Gertie was the best lady I ever knew and will ever know. It didn't matter what time of day I'd show up at her house, she was always very hospitable. She loved to have company and I loved her company even more.

Aunty Gertie was the type of lady that made a "big fuss" over you as soon as you walked through her door. She made you feel right at home. She made sure the bed was made up when she knew I was spending the night and in the morning she made the best fried egg sandwich. I am going to really miss her kind gentle ways of saying I love you. I have so many great memories of Aunty Gertie, a lady I'm proud to call my *Nonny.*

Memories by Art Collison

To Gertie with loving gratitude. When you love someone you will receive love because love always returns to itself. It is with humble recognition that we have been helped by others, as Gertie has done so many times in her life through her loving tender kindness and caring soul. She was kind to everyone she encountered in her life. Her marriage began in the hearts of both partners. One loves the partner as one loves oneself with equal love. Marriage is a journey of becoming fully present to oneself and the other; marriage is a vow that is renewed each moment. Gertie is on her journey to the land of souls to join her loving husband. The one she honored and loved in life and after life. She made one commitment to one man and she joins her husband who was her love on earth and for all eternity.

Many grateful people want to return the kindness and they want to lift up those that are feeling the loss of a loved one. Life's empty, unless it includes giving to others as Gertie has done. But to be grateful for all our lives, the good as well as the bad, the moments of joy, moments of sorrow, successes, failures, rewards as well as the rejections. *Howa* to all for showing your love for our loving mother, mother-in-law, *Nonny,* Aunty, and friend. It's worth remembering that giving thanks is so simple. It is the humble recognition that we have helped others. Now the great soaring eagle has come to take Gertie White to be with her loved ones who are waiting for her in heaven.

Memories by Ben White

I will always cherish the memories I had with Mom. I will never forget the many words of advice she gave me. She said, "I know how to do everything." I was always so happy she liked to stay with me in Prince Rupert. She loved to stay with me and I'm so proud and honoured that I have these special moments with my mom. She will always be in my heart.

The hardest thing in our life is to loose our dear precious Mother. She was the connection to our extended family. She was our mentor, our role model. She was our teacher and advisor.

Mom loved all of us unconditionally. When we needed help or constructive criticism, Mom was always there to give us direction and give us a different point of view. She loved all her grandchildren, great grandchildren, nieces, and nephews. They gave her a reason to live and enjoy life. Our mother was an elegant woman. She always dressed in her finest clothes and she presented herself elegantly in public gatherings and her daily life. She set a fine example for us to follow and carry on. She worked hard all her life. Mom has had a long life and she was ready to go to the land of souls. She was a strong powerful Haida woman and she leaves behind a great legacy for her family and *Tsath Lanas* clan. Our mother is not suffering or in pain anymore. She is safe in the arms of Jesus. We all love our mother and we will miss her dearly.

Frog Design

My Precious Children

Kaakuns was always surrounded by her large extended family all her life. She has numerous cousins and relatives living on Haida Gwaii, and they have extended family members living all over in different countries and cities. Her grandmother had three sons and three daughters. Her mother had five sons and two daughters. Her mother's sister, Jessie had eighteen children. Her brother, Paul White Jr. has seven children. She always looked forward with great anticipation of having many of her own children. But life does not turn out the way we plan it. When she was young she always thought she would have a huge family like her Aunty Jessie Hamilton. This is Kaakuns story.

During my first eight years of marriage, my husband and I became extremely worried and over anxious about having our own children. During those eight years, I went to several different doctors to find out why I couldn't conceive. I had three different tests and one operation. I even took the fertility pill for one year in great expectation; I would be blessed with a child. But the fertility pill did not work. Test after test I took ended in tears, agony, and frustration.

The final disappointment was when I went to Vancouver to have another test. The doctor did not give me any medication prior to the examination. I put my trust in the doctor in hopes of ending eight years of childlessness. The end result of the examination was dreadfully painful. I felt the doctor examining me, but my body was full of pain and my body felt so cold. Ironically sweat was dripping down my forehead and my tears were mixed in with my sweat. After the examination, the nurse didn't even have the compassion or professional courtesy to assist me in dressing.

It felt like I was lying on the examination table for hours. My whole body was weak. I was alone, without my family or husband to help me. I tried persistently to get up, but my body was too weak. Finally, I was able to regain my strength and dress myself. As I lay in my hotel room, I made a promise I will never go for any more tests again. This was the ultimate of pain and suffering that I experienced in my attempts to resolve this unfortunate barren situation.

Grief and panic over took my emotions and I went to visit my grandmother. I told her about all the pain I experienced trying to find out why I couldn't have children. *Nonny* Amanda said in the Haida language, "I will give you some medicine to clean out your body system." She went to get devil's club. *Nonny* said, "The Haida people have been using devil's club for thousands of years. Long before the white man doctors came to our land." *Nonny* said, "The Haida people use this medicine when our body is in pain. We use it for arthritis, stomach ulcers and many other ailments." She said, "Our people use the roots to relieve pain from insect bites, stings, toothaches, and skin irritations. The important thing is to know when to pick the medicine and how to make the medicine."

She continued and said, "I will make you some medicine. It will clean the inside of your body." She made the medicine a certain way and she told me to take an appropriate amount of medicine everyday. I listened to *Nonny* and I took the medicine everyday. Four months later, I announced the grandest news to my husband and family. "I'm pregnant!" *Nonny* said, "You have to take care of your body while you are pregnant. Don't smoke, don't drink and take a walk everyday." I took *Nonny's* advice and I walked three miles up to New Massett everyday. Sometimes, I walked on the beach to get exercise and I looked for agates. Finally, the day came when my precious daughter was born.

She was born on November 3, 1986. My mom, *Nonny*

Amanda, Aunty Jessie, and Aunty Dorothy Bell were there to witness the birth of my daughter. My sister-in-law, Mary Ethel White was of great assistance to me. She made me focus on my breathing, which is very important when I went into labor. One thing that was so amazing was I had very little pain during my delivery because I took daily walks and drank lots of water to nourish my body and nourish my baby.

When the doctor gently handed my daughter to me, I was ecstatic and overjoyed. I told Mom right away that I am going to name my daughter Stolly, after my sister. I knew in my heart and soul that I wanted to name my newly born daughter Stolly. The English translation for Stolly means "Dear One." My husband was excited when he heard the news. Unfortunately, he could not be there. He was working for Husby Forest Products on *Tsathlanas* land at Naden Harbour. He is always working. He works very hard to support our family. He was overjoyed to hear the grand news. We had a new-born daughter. After the birth of my daughter, my life changed. I had a new meaning and outlook on life. My life surrounded my daughter's schedule. I became a more open minded and happy person because I was blessed with my precious little daughter. My step children all loved their little sister and always took care of her.

The number *four* is a significant number for the Haida people. Four represents the four directions of wind. (north, south, east, and west). The number four is significant for the four seasons and the four holistic elements of our life. The elements are physical, mental, emotional, and spiritual. It is also significant in the four traditional values which our parents taught us when we were growing up. They taught us how to respect ourselves, love our families, and understand other people's opinions and to show compassion for other people. It was four months after I started taking the Haida medicine that I conceived my daughter, Stolly. It's like a miracle because it was *four* years later I was blessed with my precious son.

My husband was there to witness the birth of our son and he cut his son's umbilical cord. During my son's birth, I was not cognisant of the people in the delivery room. I was concentrating on breathing correctly. I was grateful I had my sister-in-law's help again to focus on my breathing. My husband was holding my hands and Dr. Deagle delivered my baby and said, "It's a boy." I was overjoyed to hear that I had a son. When the doctor took our son to clean him up, I turned around. I saw my mom, Auntie Jessie, Ben Penna, Edison Wilson, and my nephew Jayson White. They came to witness the birth of my son. It was one of the most joyous moments I had in my life to give birth to my children and to be surrounded with my family. They silently gave me their love, support, and prayers.

My husband had the honor to name our son and he gave him a Haida name, Tatzen. It means "The Haida spirits are always alive." Tatzen was born on March 23, 1991. Both my children were born at Massett, B.C. in the lands of Haida Gwaii, among the spirits of our great ancestors.

My children have changed my life. They give me inspiration to carry on my goals and aspirations. Everyday, I see my children growing, laughing, crying and calling me the magic word, "Mom." I reflect back to the years I was married and I often think of how lonely my life would be without my children. I thank our Creator for blessing me with my children and I thank my grandmother for sharing her incredible Haida knowledge and healing medicines with me. I thank our Creator for giving me a grandmother who was so wise and knowledgeable. *Nonny* was born in a generation of wise Elders. She grew up in the Haida culture, beliefs, customs, language, and traditions.

My husband, Art and I will be married for thirty one years on March 10, 2010. We are truly blessed with the riches of our children. Stolly and Tatzen give us a reason to live. They give us energy, motivation, inspiration, and love. I am very fortunate to be blessed with four step-children: Arthur, Brock, Erica, and Jolene. It is a joy and blessing for Art and I to watch our children grow and mature everyday.

Every opportunity, I say a silent prayer and thank *Nonny*

Amanda for teaching me the ways of our great Haida ancestors. *Nonny* Amanda died on July 30, 1987, at the age of eighty-three. But, I am happy she was still alive to see her great granddaughter, Stolly. Unfortunately, she died before my son was born, but my son Tatzen will know and love his great grandmother through the powerful legacy she has left behind. Every time I look at my children, I know I am a very lucky lady to be blessed with my own precious children.

Eagle Feather Design

Beliefs of the Haida People

In the Haida culture, we have many beliefs. Many of these beliefs have been passed down from each generation. Some of the beliefs may sound bizarre and out of the ordinary. Some of our beliefs are part of our survival; they teach us how to prevent illness and make medicinal cures. Some beliefs are to scare away bad spirits. Each culture has their beliefs. Some people believe that if you walk under a ladder or a black cat runs across your path, you will have bad luck. Other cultures believe that you must always wear a hat to cover your hair. The Haida people have a spiritual belief that all the plants, animals, trees, rivers, and mountains - all of Mother Earth - have a spirit. We believe every human being has a soul. We believe we all have a spirit. We believe we must learn to respect Mother Earth and Mother Nature to have a balance in the environment and in our lives.

The First Nations people of the Northwest Coast have many different beliefs. Some of the beliefs of the Haida, Tsimshian, and Nisga'a are similar. Many of the beliefs may sound very strange to non-native people. My grandmother used to tell me many of the Haida beliefs when I was a young girl. Some beliefs are frightening and some beliefs are rather amusing and humorous.

One of the beliefs teaches us that the Haida men must leave some of the meat and salmon behind when they go out hunting and fishing in order to have more animals and salmon the following year. They purified themselves by drinking and bathing in devil's club. The men had to prepare themselves mentally, physically, and spiritually before they go out hunting and fishing. Ghosts and animals do not like filth or unclean people. This is one of the reasons why the men bath in devil's club. They remove the human smell and they are successful hunters and fishermen.

Another belief holds that we must leave behind a gift for the land when we are travelling throughout our homelands. An example is when my sister, Rose Bell was kayaking throughout the lands of Haida Gwaii. She was grateful and appreciated the gifts that Mother Nature provided for all our people. She travelled everywhere on the islands and she left a gift behind. Sometimes she left behind beautiful colourful agates or an eagle feather to thank the great spirits for taking care of the land.

Nonny Amanda told me a particularly personal belief about what our great ancestors believed happened to a person who drowned. I often think about this particular belief because it affects my life so deeply. My father was our protector and provider. He worked hard all his life and he was a successful fisherman. He was always proud of himself in his accomplishments in building his own boat and building his own house. He was very kind and he was always willing to share the salmon with the extended family members and friends. Many of the people were always grateful for the salmon because they couldn't go out to get salmon. The reason why this particular belief affected my life so much is because my Dad drowned. He didn't drown in the fishing grounds. He fell off the wharf while he was repairing his boat. Some of the Haida people believe when a person drowns their spirit turns into a whale. *Nonny* Amanda said this was true in the older days of our great ancestors. Today, I always wonder about this belief. Every time I go home on the ferry to Haida Gwaii, I always see a whale.

Beyond these beliefs there are also spiritual beliefs that the Haida hold dear. This is a story my grandmother heard when she was a girl. Long ago, there were two Haida brothers who went out hunting. While they were out hunting, they came across several killer whales. The killer whales invited the two brothers down to enter the house of killer whales in the deep ocean. They stayed in the killer whales' house for a long time. Soon the eldest brother transformed into a killer whale. The younger brother did not transform into a killer whale. After a long time he escaped. When he escaped and reached his home, he told his family what happened to his older brother.

Many days passed and he missed his brother and yearned for his company. Then one night his spirit left his body, and he went out hunting with his brother that transformed into a killer whale. While his spirit was out hunting with his older brother, his body remained in the longhouse. Every time they went out hunting, the next day their mother and father would find a big whale on the beach. The two brothers went out hunting for many months and they brought back plenty of seafood for their family. One day, the younger brother felt great sadness in his heart. He knew something was wrong with his older brother. The next day he went outside and found the body of a killer whale lying on the beach. The younger brother knew the killer whale was his brother. He told his mother and father about what happened to their eldest son, and he told them how they went out hunting together. They loved their son so much that they built a big grave house for the son who turned into a killer whale.

Another belief is about when children pretend to cry. The Elders have always told us to stop the children when they pretend to cry. Sometimes when the young children are playing around and they pretend to cry, the Elders would scold them and tell them to quite pretending to cry. The Elders believe it is not good. If the children pretend to cry, something bad will happen. Some of these beliefs are very frightening. Some people think these are foolish things to believe in. We never questioned our Elders because they are teaching us valuable lessons.

The Elders use devil's club for protection and to cure many illnesses. The devil's club has a prickly outer bark and it is very potent medicine. The person who makes the medicine must have experience and knowledge in preparing the devil's club. Many of the Haida people believe that devil's club is the most powerful and potent medicine. They also use the devil's club for good luck. Eagles and humming birds are also a sign of good luck. However, birds also bring bad news. When a bird hits a window, this signifies something negative will happen.

Another belief is about reincarnation. The primary means of reincarnation is when a person has a dream about a loved one that has travelled to the land of souls. They dream about this loved one just prior to the birth of a child. This means the new born child is reincarnated and will have physical or similar behavior traits as the loved one that has passed away. In the Haida language we call this *hunch.*

There is one belief that is rather funny. When a person makes a sound from inside their throat, our people believe that someone is thinking about them. When I make this sound I say, "I wonder who is thinking about me? I hope they are thinking good thoughts." Often when I make this sound, I always say, "My mother is thinking of me even when she is in heaven."

There is another belief when a person is wishing for certain food. There is a feeling inside their mouth that doesn't go away until they eat this specific food. I like to eat all the seafood, but my favourite seafood is fried razor clams and smoked sockeye. When I am wishing for fried razor clams, the feeling inside my throat doesn't go away until I eat the clams or smoked sockeye. One day, my cousin Audra Collison brought some razor clams from Haida Gwaii for us to eat while it was fresh. I thought about eating the clams all night and I decided to get up early in the morning, clean the clams, and have them for breakfast. However I did not know that my husband had similar plans. He woke up at six o'clock in the morning to fry the clams and he ate up all the best part of the clams called the "boots." I called him a "greedy raven."

The Elders always told the young boys not to wear hats in the house; if they do then they will loose their hair and go bald. In our language we call this *skajuu.*

These are only some of our beliefs. Every culture has their beliefs. Some of them may sound foolish, scary, or outrageous. Each diverse First Nations and cultural groups have the right to believe or not believe in their customs and beliefs.

Raven Design

Golden Spruce

The Golden Spruce is a young Haida boy that turned into a tree. The Haida people call the golden spruce Kiid K'iyaas *which means the Old Tree. The Old tree is located on the beautiful mystical Islands of Haida Gwaii in a place called Yakoun Valley. The Haida Elders have passed this story onto each generation for over three centuries. My grandmother told me this story in the year 1962. Kate Gulaay Bell told her daughter, Amanda Edgars this story in the year 1909. This story was told to Kate Gulaay Bell in 1858 by her grandmother, Mary Kaakuns Bell. There are many versions and variations of this story. I want to share this version of the story of the young Haida boy because this story was passed on to each generation of Haida women. This story is important to share from a Haida perspective through our voice. It is time for us to write our stories from our point of view.*

A long time ago, there was a young Haida boy who lived in a village at *Yakoun* valley. The young boy came from the Raven clan. His grandfather was a wise and kind man. He taught him many skills. He taught the young boy how to hunt for deer and catch salmon and how to survive. He taught him how to preserve food for the long winter season. The young boy caught plenty of sockeye at *Yakoun* River and he dried the sockeye. His grandfather taught him many traditional values, customs, and beliefs of the Haida people. But sometimes the young boy did not listen.

One day, during the winter time the young Haida boy needed to go use the bathroom, but he didn't want to walk down to the river. It was too cold and the frosty wind was blowing against his face. He was too lazy to walk to the river. So he used the bathroom close to their longhouse. When he finished relieving himself, he started laughing and laughing at his droppings because it was so cold that it froze and it looked just like a tree. The young boy didn't listen to his grandfather who taught him how to respect nature. The boy continued laughing and showing his disrespect to nature's way.

The spirits of nature heard the young boy making fun of nature. Soon it began to snow. It snowed every day. It continued to snow for many days. Soon all the people in the village were afraid; they did not understand why it was snowing so hard. The snow covered the roofs of their longhouses and soon they could barely leave their homes. Many of the people brought their wood supply into the longhouses, but soon the wood supply and some of the food started to run out. Then the water supply started running out. They could not leave their houses because the snow was too thick. They could not dig through the snow, to go to the river for water. They could not share the food resources with their cousins and relatives. The younger people who lived in one longhouse shared their food with the children and Elders.

After many weeks, the children began to become very weak and ill. Many of the children were dying of starvation and illness. The wood supply and food rations soon ran out. Many of the people were dying of starvation and from the bitter cold. The snow did not stop and soon it covered the entire village. After many months, all the people died, except the old grandfather and the young boy. Finally the young boy started to dig a tunnel through the snow to reach the top of the longhouse.

The young boy dug for many days. His grandfather was too weak to help him dig but he encouraged the young boy to keep digging. The young Haida boy dug for hours and days until finally he could see the bright blue sky above. When he reached the top of the snow, he yelled at his grandfather to climb up and see the bright sky. The grandfather was very weak and tired, but he was happy to hear they could finally escape from being trapped in their longhouse.

They both climbed above the snow and they could see the brightness of life surrounding their village. The sun was shining and the birds were chirping. The trees were glistening from the bright sun shining in the clear blue sky. The animals were sparkling with life in the whole valley. The grandfather and his grandchild felt free and happy to be alive. They started walking down to the river. They had to find another place to build their new home. While they were walking down to the river, his grandfather told the boy not to look back at their lost village. The grandfather told him the spirits of nature will come and take him into their world.

The young boy thought about what he did. He realized that he did not listen to his grandfather's words of advice when he started laughing at nature. He was heartbroken about losing his family. He felt awful about losing his friends and home. He knew that he should listen to his grandfather and he should not look back, but his sadness of losing his family and home overcame him. He felt dreadful about leaving the only home he knew. He felt sad about the great loss of his family. He felt the tears in his eyes and his heart was pounding and great waves of sadness flashed through his heart. Then he looked back for one final glance at his lost village and family.

When he looked back, the spirits of nature swiftly grabbed the young boy's feet. He could not move. He yelled to his grandfather to stop and help him, but soon the young boy's feet were rooted to the ground. He yelled and cried for help. But his feet were growing right into the earth. His grandfather tried to help him and pulled with all his power, but the young boy could not move. The grandfather knew that he must leave his grandson. In sadness and with a heavy heart, the grandfather told his grandson he must leave him. When the grandfather was leaving, he told his grandson that he will live as the Old Tree until the end of the world. He told his grandson that many people will stop and admire the Haida boy who lives as a tree.

All the people will learn how to respect nature and treat the land and trees with the greatest of respect. The Old Tree will live for eternity. The grandfather continues his journey to find a new home. He left his grandson rooted to the earth with nature shining around him. This is how the young Haida boy lives on as the Golden Spruce.

The Loss of our Haida Ancestor

In the year 1997, Thomas Grant Hadwin, 48, publicly boasted that he cut down the Golden Spruce known as the Haida boy from *Yakoun* Valley. Grant Hadwin wrote the following:

> Re: The Falling of Your "Pet Plant" On January 20 and January 21, 1997.
>
> I put the falling cuts, into a tree, known as the Golden Spruce, near Port Clements, Queen Charlotte Islands, British Columbia. The tree is one, of two known Sitka Spruce, I believe, with an unusual colour pigmentation, which apparently causes a slightly golden hue. This tree is situated in a small "island" of old-growth forest, in a vast clear-cut, (more or less), known as Haida Gwaii, by The Haida Aboriginal People. The next storm, in Haida Gwaii (if not before) will probably cause this +1000 year old plant, to fall into or near, The *Yakoun* River.
>
> I don't care much for "freaks" whether they teach in university classrooms, sit in corporate boardrooms, perform in the circus or are put on display, as examples of old growth forest conservation or demonstration forests. I didn't enjoy butchering this magnificent old plant, but you apparently need a message and wake-up call, that even a university trained professional, should be able to understand.

I draw your attention, to the *Yukon news*, of December 11, 1996 and the *Daily News*, in Prince Rupert, of January 7, 1997. (Next to the article on the Queen Charlotte City garbage dump and the murderer and the pedophile story). Perception is everything, I'm told. I really didn't have much trouble, crossing a rain swollen *Yakoun* River, at midnight, with a chainsaw and other equipment. Swimming in the *Yakoun* River, for thirteen minutes at -30 degrees Centigrade, is more challenging. It was challenging, however, to fall a +2 metre diameter Golden, at night, with a 25 inch chainsaw bar and leave this large plant, in a temporary vertical position.

I mean no disrespect, to most of the Haida People, by my actions or to the natural environment, of Haida Gwaii. I do however; mean this action, to be an expression, of my rage and hatred, towards university trained professionals and their extreme supporters, whose ideas, ethics, denials, part truths, attitudes etc. appear to be responsible, for most of the abominations, towards amateur life, on this planet.

Unfortunately, institutional professionals appear to be insane, in varying degrees, perhaps due in part, to economically and psychologically abusive training methods. Please find enclosed, some of the last known photographs, of the Golden Spruce (unless you hurry), before the next wind storm.

Yours truly
Grant Hadwin

This reprint is word for word, of the letter Grant Hadwin sent to MacMillan Bloedel, Greenpeace and the Haida Nation, as well as to several individuals and other groups. *The Observer* prints it as a matter of public record (*The Observer*, January 30, 1997).

There are many different versions of the Golden Spruce story written in various newspapers. However, the reporters do not indicate who told these versions. *The Daily News* printed the following version:

> Haida oral tradition on the Golden Spruce predates written history and relates to the legend of a grandson who disobeyed his grandfather, the only two survivors of a summer snowstorm. Legend has it that the village people were speaking ill of each other. They ended up trapped in their homes due to the snow, unable to get firewood and food. The old man and grandson were able to survive under a cedar mat until a bird came to them with a seed to show all was well. As the pair were leaving the village, the boy was told not to look back. He did, grew roots and became *K'iid K'iyaas.*

In the same article there is another version as follows:

> The Legend says the tree would be seen by all, until the last people. Those who saw the tree down centuries ago feared they were the last people until the new golden spruce grew at the spot. As hope for regrowth fuels the Haida, they are also seeking consequences. (Colpitts, *The Daily News,* January 26, 1997)

Another version of the story was written in *Raven's Eye* newspaper as follows:

> The Haida people have passed on a story through the generations about the tree, explaining its spiritual value to the culture: *Kiidkayaas*, a Haida boy and his grandfather were the lone survivors of a very severe snowstorm. As they sadly left their traditional home to join with another community, the grandfather warned the youngster not to look back. But the boy couldn't help himself. When he turned to look he became rooted to the ground and transformed into

the tree. (Barnslet, *Raven's Eye Newspaper,* May 1997)

On January 23, 1997, a press release from the Council of the Haida Nation, Vernon Brown, and President stated the following:

> The Haida people are saddened and angered by the destruction of *K'iid K'iyaas* (Old Tree), also known as the "Golden Spruce," in the *Yakoun* River Valley on Haida Gwaii. The loss of *K'iid K'iyaas* is a deliberate violation of our cultural history. Our oral traditions about *K'iid K'iyaas* predate written history. We declare to the world that the Haida Nation takes full ownership of the remains *K'iid K'kiyaas,* and that it is declared off limits to everyone. The Haida will conduct a private ceremony at the site to reconcile the loss. The Haida expect that Justice will prevail and that the person responsible for the act of destruction will be punished. The Haida people will be watching every detail and if there is no apparent justice, the Haida will take appropriate action. The Haida have long regarded *K'iid K'iyaas* as a sentinel of the *Yakoun* Valley, and now that it has been destroyed, the Haida's will escalate protectionist measures for our land.

On May 1997, the headlines printed by *Raven's Eye* The newspaper stated the following:

> The crew of the RCMP patrol boat Inkster continue the search for the man accused of cutting down a golden spruce considered sacred by the Haida people. Grant Hadwin, 48, was released on his own recognisance last January after being charged with mischief to property in connection with the felling of the rare conifer.
>
> When he failed to appear for his first appearance

> in provincial court on Feb 18, a warrant was issued for his arrest. "Mr. Hadwin was last believed to be paddling his way towards the Queen Charlotte Islands, which means that the patrol boat section is conducting the investigation," RCMP Corporal Grant Wilson told Raven's Eye. (*Raven's Eye Newspaper,* May 1997)

There is a lot of speculation about what happened to Grant Hadwin. To this day in the year 2010, he has not been found to face these charges.

Tribute to the Haida Boy

I pay tribute to the young Haida boy who lived for over three hundred years as the Golden Spruce. He stood tall to remind the Haida people in each generation to never give up their land and identity. He reminded the Haida people to respect others and to respect mother earth. I believe he wanted the Haida people to treat the land and nature with the utmost respect and to keep the lands of Haida Gwaii intact for their future generations. He wanted this generation to follow the example of how our great Haida ancestors fought to protect the lands of Haida Gwaii for thousands of years.

Everyone has different perspectives of the Golden Spruce. It is important to write my point of view. The following is my perspective of what I believe and how I pay tribute to the Golden Spruce. I believe the Golden Spruce witnessed how the Haida people flourished and took great care of the land for centuries. He watched the Haida people become powerful people by respecting each clan's territories and how they respected the lands of Haida Gwaii. He watched as they took only what they needed and observed how they shared their food and resources with each other. The young boy was indeed proud of all the people for sharing and caring for one another.

I believe the young boy known as the Golden Spruce has silent testimony of how the non-natives came to the lands of Haida Gwaii. He watched how the disease called the smallpox killed the Haida people by the thousands. This was one of the most devastating parts of our history, when our ancestors did not understand why the Haida people were dying. The young boy silently witnessed centuries of discriminating history. He witnessed how the Indian Agents took away the children to residential schools. The residential schools are an example of cultural genocide. The intent was to assimilate the children and take away their language, culture, and families as a whole.

Today, the majority of our people cannot speak the Haida language. The negative experiences of the residential schools had a lasting effect on many of the children's lives. Many people experienced the trauma of separation from their families and could not speak their own languages at the residential schools. After many years there are still Haida people who are suffering from the verbal, sexual, physical, and emotional abuse they experienced at residential schools. This evident abuse has lingered in many families and individuals for several generations.

Today there are individuals who are healing themselves in many different ways. Some of the Haida people are using the Indian medicines and practices to heal their pains, sorrows, and broken spirits. The young boy witnessed how many of the Haida people and First Nations people survived the assaults and discrimination of the *Indian Act* enacted in 1876. (see *Indian Act*, 1984) He witnessed how the *Indian Act* refused First Nations people the rights to vote. The only way they could vote is when they applied to become enfranchised. This meant that when a First Nation person applied to lose their status and rights under the *Indian Act*, they were allowed to vote or go to university.

The young boy witnessed how the federal legislation continued to dictate the *Indian Act*. In the year 1890 the *Indian Act* banned the potlatch system and the practice of feasts and winter dance ceremonials. The potlatches and feasts are part of our social, cultural, and political lives. At these events the Haida people confirmed their leadership and recognized the property and territorial rights of each Hereditary Chief. The potlatch is part of our social system where people witness and validate a specific occasion such as naming a Hereditary Chief or other name-giving events, affirming oral histories and clan territories, and displaying crests of the Haida people.

The Haida boy also witnessed when the First Nations people had no say in how their properties would be distributed or inherited when they died without a will. When a First Nations person dies without a will, the federal government appoints a representative to execute their belongings and personal property. The *Indian Act* implemented legislation called Bill C-31 to discriminate against First Nations woman. When a First Nations woman married a non-native person, she lost her status as a registered Indian. These are a few examples of how our lives were controlled and manipulated and how the *Indian Act* impacted negatively on our traditions and culture.

I believe that throughout history, the Haida boy has witnessed the Haida leaders speaking out against the *Indian Act*. Our great grandfathers have spoken against the appalling destruction of our resources and lands and the placement of our people on small reserves. Many First Nations leaders have continued to speak about the cultural genocide enacted by the residential school system. I believe the Haida boy witnessed generations of social and family dysfunctions caused by the residential school systems and *Indian Act*. These are examples of the most discriminating piece of legislation ever produced in history against the Haida people and First Nations people.

The young Haida boy also witnessed positive aspects of the Haida Nation when they worked together to build their longhouses and shared their food with their extended family members. He witnessed how the Haida people learned their culture and traditions and utilized all the resources for medicinal values and used the cedar bark, roots, and wood for weaving and carving. He was proud of the Haida people who are famous and renowned as the greatest totem pole and canoe carvers in history. He observed many young Haida men who carved out of the black stone called *argillite.* Our people have an added distinction as the only First Nations people who carve out of the beautiful black argillite. He observed as many young men continue to display their talents in carving elaborate beautiful totem poles and exquisite carvings in wood, argillite, gold, and silver. The Haida art is the hallmark of our people and they continue to be known throughout the world through their remarkable artwork.

In every story there is always a positive and negative aspect. Naturally there are some people who do not believe the story of the little boy who turned into the golden spruce. Some people called the golden spruce "M & B's pet tree." Others called this an outright murder of a young Haida boy. Some people said, if the Golden Spruce dies, the Haida Nation will die too. Obviously, this statement is not true because we have a strong Nation of Haida people still living today. We are proud of our culture and identity. We are a living testimony that the Haida Nation is still strong and alive. The Haida people will live for many more generations to carry on the traditions and customs of our great ancestors.

One of the most respected leaders of Haida Gwaii is the Late Ernie Collison. Many people knew him as "Big Eagle." His Haida name is Skilay. In my opinion Ernie was one of the most dynamic, energetic, and respected man from Haida Gwaii. "When a journalist asked Skilay if he really believed a little boy could turn into a tree, he retorted, "Do you believe a woman could turn into a block of salt?'" (Vaillant, 2005, p. 149)

Many of the Haida Elders and non-natives living on Haida Gwaii were crying for the loss of the young Haida boy. The Haida people held a memorial service to mourn one of our ancestors. This is a sorrowful heartbreaking feeling. It is similar to losing one of our own family members. My heart was heavy with sadness when my mom phoned me to tell me that the Golden Spruce was cut down. Mom said, "Aunty Dorothy Bell and lots of the Haida people were crying and heartbroken about loosing the Golden Spruce." The loss is the same feelings I had when my dad, brother, and sister died. Any person who experiences the loss of a loved one will understand the feelings of how the Haida people felt when Grant Hadwin killed the young Haida boy known as the Golden Spruce.

Some people believe there will always be a Big Tree. They believe when the tree grows too old, another tree will grow. I remember *Nonny* Amanda saying "This happened to a young Haida boy; if this happened to a young Haida girl, there would be thousands of golden spruce trees all over Haida Gwaii because the girl is the one who has the children." There are many different beliefs and versions of the Golden Spruce. I tend to believe the Haida Elders and my grandmother's version of the story. This story was passed down from my great great grandmother, Mary Guulay Bell in 1858. She was *Nonny's* grandmother. During those days, the oldest living relative of the grandfather and young Haida boy was Agnes Williams. Agnes is an elegant elder who comes from *Yakoun* Valley.

The death of the Haida boy took a toll on many Haida people. Many of the Haida Elders who understood the value and importance of the Golden Spruce cried and mourned the great loss of our ancestor. The death of the Golden Spruce brought together many Haida people and residents of Haida Gwaii. I believe it is important I quote parts of a sermon preached by Reverend Peter Hamel: "We were all shocked this week to learn that a crazed individual had cut down the Golden Spruce. People were angry and disturbed to think that anyone would commit such a senseless act." He continued, "The perpetrator could never grasp the impact he would have on all of us here in the islands and beyond. This was not just a physical tree of unusual beauty; it was in fact a unique symbol of the islands and us. It was a mythic tree that sustained our spirits whenever we saw it." He further added, "It was a symbol, whether we recognized it or not, that we need the earth and the sunlight, the physical and the spiritual, to nourish both the body and the soul. The presence of this tree, almost more than any other living form, brought us together and lifted us from the familiar to the divine." Reverend Peter Hamel added, "The Golden Spruce was sheltered by the river in a cathedral of old growth trees. It is a sacred space for loggers, the Haida, fishermen, the military, the business community, teachers, naturalists, environmentalists, and everyone who came in sight of him. This gift from Mother Earth connected us with our deepest spiritual needs. Its senseless destruction wounded each one of us as much as the loss of its wondrous beauty in the sacred grove by the *Yakoun* River. (The *Observer,* January 30, 1997)

I know there are people from all over the world that have come to see the Golden Spruce. Every one has fond memories of the Golden Spruce. I will always remember this spiritual Golden tree standing tall with radiant golden needles shining in the brightness by the river. My mother, Gertie White told me about how her sisters used to go see the Golden Spruce. They talked in their own language and told each other stories about their younger days. The tree in its golden silence brought them together as a family. They always felt a sense of "peace" when they went to visit the Golden Spruce.

Perhaps someday the person responsible will get his justice for destroying part of our legacy and destroying part of our culture. I believe someday the spirits of our great ancestors will give rebirth to this sacred tree, which is a symbol of our Haida history and part of our spiritual being. One of our beliefs and traditions is called reincarnation. In the Haida language, we call it *hunch.* Perhaps, some day the Golden Spruce will be reincarnated and the young Haida boy will once again stand proud to always remind our people to empower themselves to stand strong as the Haida Nation and continue to protect the lands of Haida Gwaii for our future generation.

Hand Salmon Design

Drum Making

The Haida people have used the drum from the beginning of time. We use drums for a spiritual connection when our loved ones have gone to the land of souls. We use drums for healing purposes and we use drums when we sing and perform at potlatches. The drums are significant for sending out messages. It is a method of communication to provide entertainment at a potlatch. When I teach the art of drum making, the students are encouraged to have a positive attitude. It is important to have respect and patience when anyone is making a drum.

Drums have been part of the Haida culture since time immemorial. The spiritual component of the drum is very important to the Haida people. The drum and drumming is a spiritual connection to the loved ones that have passed onto the spirit world. For example, when I sing the Spirit song, I beat the drum in a slow beating sound. I am singing the song and beating the drum in a slow drumming rhythm to "clean the air" and open our heart to celebrate this special occasion. The drum sound carries the message to each person in the hall and makes them feel welcome and makes their hearts feel at ease. The drum beats with power and conviction sending out a message and grasping the attention of everyone to stop and listen to the message of the drum and the strong message of the spirit song.

Some of the Haida traditions and values are different from other First Nations groups. The traditions or protocol of some First Nations groups, houses, or clans do not allow women to drum. The Haida people allow us to drum and sing Haida songs. I have been singing and drumming since I was twelve years old. The drum has different significance for each song I sing. I remember when I sang the Mourning song for my late grandfather. My heart was filled with grief, but I had to sing the song and beat the drum as the pallbearers carried the coffin down to the cemetery. I was beating the drum softly and slowly. The drum sound sent out a sad message for the loss of our grandfather. When all the people were walking down to the cemetery, I was drumming a soft slow rhythm. This was to pay our respects to a kind, loving Haida man who has travelled to the land of souls.

Drumming is also used for healing. When a person is sick, we use the drum to sing songs for healing. I sing a song called the Medicine song. My grandmother taught our dancers how to perform the dance with a medicine man song. The medicine man uses a rattle when he is dancing. When I am singing the Medicine song, I beat a fast drum rhythm. The medicine man is performing a dance and using the rattles to make the child well. When the child is healed, the dancers rejoice and dance around the young child. I continue to sing the Medicine man song and I change the rhythm of the drum to a loud fast drumming beat to signify the child has regained his health.

When I am teaching students and adults how to make a drum, it is important to listen to my directions. When a person is making a drum, they must clean their minds and be honored to make a drum. If a person does not understand any part of making a drum or they become frustrated, I ask them to put the drum down and take a break. The Elders believe if a person is getting frustrated when they are making a drum they must stop immediately. The same strategy is used when I am teaching students how to weave a basket or how to sew a button blanket. When a person is getting frustrated or discouraged, they must take a break and return when they feel they have confidence in completing the task. We believe when a person is making a drum or weaving a hat, they must put in positive energy and make the drum with pride, integrity, and honor. The drum will speak and make the person feel proud of their accomplishments when they have completed making the drum.

Materials:

- Deer skin or rawhide
- Scissors
- Lace or deer skin cut into lace
- Wooden frame (octagon shape or round shape)
- Awl to make the holes in rawhide
- Pencil to mark holes

Instructions:

Cut and measure rawhide. Soak thick rawhide overnight. Soak thin rawhide for one hour. Measure half an inch from the outer part of the drum and measure half an inch to mark the drum. Use the awl to cut the holes. Put the deer skin on to the frame. Start to lace each hole on the deer skin. Begin on the rough side and insert the lace into each hole, starting on the bottom side and continue this same procedure until all the holes have been laced. Pull the lacing to tighten the lace all around the drum. Press the palm of your hand in the centre of the drum. Press the deer skin half way into the centre and begin lacing the drum from top to bottom. Tie lace in the centre and cross to the opposite side of the drum. Repeat this procedure. Tie the remaining lace in the centre of the drum to use as a handle.

The lacing is different for each person. I teach students how to use the dream catcher method for lacing. The measurements may be more than one inch. When you press your palm in the centre of the drum, this pressure will determine the sound of the drum. When the drum is dry, the drum sound will either be a high or low sound. When I am teaching how to make drums to students or teachers, I prefer to use the round drum frames. I also prefer to cut the deer skin to cover and overlap the entire drum. Another method is to cut the deer skin to cover only half of the drum frame with no overlapping.

When the drum is laced, dry the deer skin over night. When it is dry the students can proceed to draw their crest on the drum. Students trace or draw their crest design on the drum and paint the design. This is the method I use to teach the wonderful art of drum making.

I teach the art of drum making at teachers' workshops and high schools to both adults and students. One year I travelled to Massett and I taught thirty-two students at G.M. Dawson High School how to make drums. This was a full two-day workshop. The students did an excellent job in making their drums. At the end of the session, I explained the significance of drums and we all sang Haida songs.

I also taught Mrs. L. Leach's class at Conrad Elementary School how to make drums. This specific project took over a week for the students to make the drums. This class did a remarkable job. At the end of the drum making sessions, I taught the students two Haida songs. All the students were so proud of themselves. They performed a splendid drum rhythm and sang two Haida songs at a school assembly, and the local newspaper reporter came to take pictures of Mrs. L. Leach's class displaying their beautiful drums.

I travel around to various communities to teach the art of drum making. When I see the smile and beam of excitement on the students and adults faces, I know they are proud of their accomplishments in making their own drum.

Button Blankets

The Haida people use button blankets to display their Clan crests. Each crest and emblem is a powerful statement to identify our family and clan. Our crests also identify where our territorial lands are located on Haida Gwaii. When I make a button blanket I sew the eye part on last. When I sew the eye part on my button blanket, the Eagle opens up its eyes and thanks me for keeping our traditions and culture alive. When I wear my button blanket I wear it with utmost respect.

The Haida people use button blankets for many special occasions such as name-giving potlatches, memorial potlatches, or totem pole raisings. The button blanket is a powerful statement of who we are as Haida people. In the modern world we have a driver's license and picture identification. In the Haida culture, we use our crests to symbolize and identify which clan we come from. Every person follows their mother's clan. This is called a matrilineal system. For example: My mother is from the eagle clan. Therefore, I follow my mother's lineage and clan. My son and daughter will therefore be under my clan. Each clan has many different crests. Our clan has seven different crests. We wear our button blankets to show our family emblems.

In the days of our ancestors, the button blankets, crests and names were very important and valuable to the Haida Elders. They would not allow anyone to wear their crests. It was forbidden for another clan to take their names. When a person sold their button blankets, it was just like selling their birthright or selling their identification. This is how much our ancestors respected our traditions and identity.

When I was fifteen years old, *Nonny* Amanda taught me how to make traditional button blankets, vests, capes, and dancing regalia. The first lesson I learned in how to make a button blanket was to *observe. Nonny* told me to watch how she measures and cuts the materials for a blanket. Then I watched her sew the border and designs onto the blanket. I was a keen and eager learner and soon I was able to make all my own vests and dancing regalia. Some of the Haida people did not put a border along the lower edge because it would interfere with the dancers' performance. It would also interfere with the shape of the blanket and the blanket would be too heavy for the dancers.

Nonny told me to sew the buttons onto the eye part last. She said, "This is how our family believe that we are keeping our beliefs and traditions alive. When we sew on the eye part last, we believe the eyes of the eagle will open and thank us for keeping the Haida culture alive." She said, "It doesn't matter what type of design you sew on the blanket or regalia; you must always sew the eye part on last. During the days of our great grandfathers, our people used black charcoal to make the color black. They used the drippings from the clam shells to make the color white. They used the drippings from red cedar to make the color red." The traditional colours have always been red and black. In our great ancestor's days, they used animal skins and furs to make their ceremonial robes. They painted their crests on the animal skin. The Haida people with high rank used sea otter fur for the border. They also wove all their clothing, capes, hats, bowls, and baskets. Today, we continue to make our elegant ceremonial button blankets and we continue to weave traditional dancing regalia.

Throughout my years as a teacher, I have taught many students and adults how to make button blankets and to have a better understanding and appreciation for the Haida culture. I have taught grade one and two classes for several years. When I was teaching grade two and three classes at Conrad Elementary School, the principal Ms. Leah Robinson approached me to plan a school-wide project to make four school banners. This was an exciting project and I made plans with the teachers to send a group of students down to my class every day where they could work on tracing, cutting, and sewing the designs. The students had the opportunity to learn the significance of the four major crests of the Tsimshian people and they learned how to sew buttons onto the border of the crests and banners. This was an exciting project where each student from Kindergarten to grade seven was able to participate in making the school banners. The banners were presented to the school and dignitaries at a school assembly witnessed the Tsimshian Elders bless the banners.

I also taught my grade two & three classes at Seal Cove Elementary School how to make mini button blankets with their First Nations crest designs. Some students did not have a crest, so they selected a butterfly or a crest of their choice for their mini button blanket. When the students were sewing the buttons on the blankets, I had to have this monitored very carefully by the childcare worker. This was a safety precaution when the students were using a sewing needle. During this period, I also utilized the Role Model program to assist in monitoring and helping the students.

When I was teaching the adults at the Friendship House, we took on a huge challenge to make the biggest banner possible to display the four major crests. The students enjoyed this project immensely and they were very proud of the banner, which is now displayed at the Friendship House boardroom.

The following directions are for a mini button blanket or adult button blanket. I have included various activities for a First Nations unit. In this unit students will be able to learn how to participate cooperatively in class activities (e.g. art projects, listening to stories and Elders). They will be able to work in small groups; gather information from parents, grandparents and Elders; and share stories of their lives and personal experiences. They will be able to demonstrate active listening skills in the classroom during morning circle or when I read

First Nations stories. Through learning how to listen, they are able to ask pertinent questions to gather information from Elders and family members. Students are able to identify and express different ways of communicating through First Nations spoken languages (Haida, Nisga'a, or Smalgyax languages). Students are able to use various pictures, sing Haida songs, perform various First Nations dances, and take part in various drama or readers theatre (e.g. drama plays I wrote in my book). During daily sharing or group discussion times (e.g. show and tell, opening exercises, circle time) include opportunities for students to participate and share their ideas and experiences. I observe students' willingness to listen to others and share their ideas and experiences with the rest of the group on a daily basis. I also observe daily their ability to treat others respectfully and take turns speaking. I collect evidence of how students are able to identify which clan they belong to and understand the make up of their own family members (e.g. family tree, clans, house). I provide daily examples of ways in which my class can cooperate in a respectful and responsible manner (e.g. sharing, taking turns, following rules, and being polite).

The following are various activities I use in a First Nations unit.

Primary School: Make a paper button blanket.
Intermediate/High School: Make a mini button blanket.
Adult and college students: Make a regular button blanket.

Materials:
Black cloth, red cloth, sewing needles, red and black thread, mother of pearl buttons, pins, iron, chalk, scissors. There is a variety of cloth to select from. I use the thick Melton cloth for durable or long lasting wear and I use felt for the border. I also use stretch polyester material and ultra suede material for the design and border. Every person has a personal choice in regards to selecting the material.

Procedure:

- Measure the length of your arms and length of your body from head to ankle.
- Cut the material.
- Measure and cut the border for the blanket. Cut six inches. Use pins to attach the border around the blanket.
- Use a sewing machine or hand-sew the border onto the blanket.
- Turn and fold the border over to the other side of the blanket.
- Iron the border and use pins to keep the borders intact. Fold the border to the opposite side. Ensure the border is ironed straight. Iron on one side at the time. When the border is ironed straight, put the pins on the edge of the border and finish ironing the border straight.
- Sew the mother of pearl buttons on the border. (Optional: sew the border or use pins).
- Trace the design using a chalk. Cut the design.
- Put the design in the centre of the blanket; put the pins on the design.
- Sew the crest design in the centre of the blanket.
- Sew buttons on the design. Sew buttons on the eye part last.

When I teach First Nations studies to students in the primary or secondary levels, I teach the art of button blanket making, weaving, drum making, crests, songs, or cultural traditions that are integral and fundamental to our culture. I cannot teach one core component without integrating the traditions and culture in the art of button blanket making. Therefore, I will include various activities that I use for teaching traditions and culture, which can be adapted or modified according to which grade level I teach. The following are various activities I teach in the First Nations studies core units:

- Arrange a field trip to a local museum. Students will have an opportunity to see the old traditional button blankets worn hundreds of years ago. They will see the different ways the blankets were made and what type of material the people used in 1800. The students write a creative story or journal entry about the field trip. Write a thank you letter to the local curator for taking the students on a tour at the museum.
- Students listen to legends, stories and myths about the First Nations people. I select a variety of books about legends, myths and stories about the aboriginal people. Students read books during quiet reading. I will read a story daily and ask probing and stimulating questions about the story. Students write about the story for a language arts exercise.
- Students make a "big book." The topic may be about blankets or crests. Students will draw pictures of each crest. Students make a class "big book." Write about aboriginal legends and stories. Laminate the books and put in the classroom and school library.
- Students complete a family tree. Research their family lineage. Students interview their parents or grandparents. Ask questions about their crest, clan, or house: Example of questions. What clan do I belong too? Does our family go by a clan or house? Where is our territory located? What is my father's crest? Do I have more than one crest? Do I go under my father or mother's crest? What is my grandparents crest? Students will gather information and write about their extended families. They will write letters to their immediate family members and extended family members. They will also visit local museums, archives or marriage registry to request information on their family history.
- Invite First Nations Elders to visit the classroom to tell stories, legends and myths. Invite Haida artists, carvers, various dance groups, members of the community, or

band council members and parents to talk about the culture and traditions. If you are located in an urban community, invite other First Nations people to compare and contrast different First Nations cultures.

- Students experiment with different types of food. Arrange a field trip to the local beach to dig clams, collect shells or agates, pick seaweed, catch crabs, or simply explore the seashore. Students can learn to cook different types of food: for example, clean crabs and cook the crabs. They can gather, collect, clean, and cook a variety of seafood. Or arrange a fieldtrip to pick berries, clean the berries, and process the berries by canning or freezing them. Make fruit from the berries or make a delicious treat for the class. Parents and childcare workers may assist in making the jam and desserts.
- Students bring different types of food to school. For example, seaweed, canned salmon, smoked sockeye, *oolican* grease, fried bread, dried halibut, herring roe on kelp, and other types of food. Students tell a story about what types of food they brought to class during sharing time and share the food with the students. Students could even make gifts to give away at the mini class potlatch.
- Students can construct various crest designs of the four major crests: Eagle, Raven, Killer Whale, Wolf. The designs can be painted; traced and colored; molded out of clay; drawn from "connect-the-dots" patterns; or made into headbands. Three dimensional crests designs can also be made by drawing the design on two pieces of construction paper, cutting out the design, stapling the edges of the two pieces of paper, and then stuffing the design with newspaper. These designs can be displayed by hanging them from the classroom ceiling.
- I teach students a Haida song called the Heart Song. Students will copy the words of the song on a white doily. Glue the white doily onto a background, color the doily on the outside border. Students will review the words of the

song and learn the actions for the song. I also teach four students how to drum the rhythm of the song and four students to shake the rattles. Each child has contributed to learning the song and actions. Students sing the song at a school assembly.

- I composed a *How-a* Song for students to sing and use actions as follows: Oh hoo I say thank you to my mommy and my daddy, I say "I love my family". In my heart forever. Way ah ha, way ah ha, way ah ha hoo.
- Put students in pairs. One student will read a First Nations story, the other is the listener. The student will read a story and the other student will listen to the story. The student will also retell the story in their own words. Switch places. Repeat the process.
- Conduct an oral discussion about the four B's: Be respectful, Be responsible, Be cooperative, and Be safe. During the morning circle, discuss various ideas and print the examples the students provided on the board about how to be respectful. Example: I will listen to the teacher when she is talking. I will listen to the students when they are talking. I will listen to the Elders when they visit our classroom. I will use "I care language." Explain the concept that hands are for helping not hurting. Ask students to provide examples of how to be safe, and how to be responsible. As a language arts activity for primary students, have them print four complete sentences in the journal entry about how to be responsible accompanied by a drawing that they can color.
- First Nations people have many traditional values such as courage, shyness, happiness, love, sharing, caring, humility, etc. Invite an Elder to the classroom to tell stories about these values. Read the story about *Tow* and *Tow-Ustasin* to understand the values of sharing and caring.
- I bring examples of my artwork: weaved hats, weaved baskets, cedar roses, mats, drums, and button blankets with various crests. I make my own vests and blazers with

Haida designs and I use my jewellery to explain different crests and designs. I sing songs and explain the significance of the drum. The students are allowed to touch the drum and smell the cedar. They record other interesting facts about the display of artwork. The students write down questions, what they know, what they don't know, and what they think they know about all my artwork. They use the strategy of the following: I think, I wonder, I know.

- Invite an Elder or local role model to the class to discuss the traditional annual activities. Write each month on a large white chart paper. Record these activities on chart paper. An example: June, collect and strip cedar bark. July, dig for clams. Students also do this as a homework project. Ask their extended family members and grandparents to assist and record what they do during each month. Compare and contrast using a Venn diagram. Record on white chart paper and display in the classroom or allow students to present their project to the class to develop their oral speaking skills.
- I always use the Queen Charlotte Islands series in providing artwork, designs, and crests. My brother Paul White Jr. is the illustrator for the book called *Haida Art*. I use this book to provide examples of crests and artwork. My sister, Rose Bell wrote the story called "The First Haida Totem Pole." I use this story in all grade levels to provide an example of how stories tell us about our history; stories are illustrated on totem poles and an introduction to celebrations of the feasts and potlatch. I use the book called *Haida Art* to discuss the crest designs and show the students the difference in Haida art and other First Nations artwork.
- I provide an opportunity for students to attend the Annual Aboriginal Days to observe various local dance groups. I also invite First Nations role models to my class to sing Tsimshian, Nisga'a, or Haida songs, and I teach the stu-

dents First Nations songs and various dance steps. An example is how I sing a Tsimshian song and Haida song together. These songs are called the entrance dances. In 2008/2009 both Ms. Skog and I used these songs at the Christmas Concert at Roosevelt Elementary School. I believe it is respectful and appropriate to sing both songs to honor both cultures. I utilize the Role Model program to invite other diverse First Nations people to come to my class to share their languages, songs, and stories in the Cree and other First Nations culture. Students may research a topic of one specific First Nations group. Write or type important facts from various books and allow students to download information from the internet. Collect various photographs from home or print from the internet to compile into a book.

- Every year I always plan a trip to watch the All Native Tournament. This is a grand basketball and cultural event which takes place in Prince Rupert every year in the month of February. In 1994, when I was teaching the Adult, Quest and Futures classes, I requested the All Native Tournament Committee to take these classes to watch a couple basketball games with the intent to interview an Elder or basketball player. Prior to going to the All Native Basketball Tournament, the students brainstormed ideas and wrote various questions for the interview. I put them in pairs to conduct an interview. At the tournament, the students had an opportunity to choose to interview a basketball player, fan, or an Elder. This was a rewarding and valuable experience for all the students, plus it was an opportunity to make new friends, enjoy eating First Nations food, and visit tables where many First Nations people were selling their creative artwork.
- Students read *The Haida Chief Who married a Kitkatla Princess* or other theatre scripts and First Nations drama plays. The topics may be about survival, creation, or transformation and could include lessons concerning tradition-

al values. Students write their own play, draw pictures, and present their play to the class.

- Use Reading Buddies. My grade two students buddy with an older student from a higher grade. Students read and listen to their buddy read First Nations stories. They share stimulating questions and make predictions. Students may also read to a younger student to build their self-confidence, word recognition, and comprehension skills.
- Collect a variety of First Nations stories that a special helper can select from to read to the class during morning circle. I also provide opportunities for students to ask questions about the specific story.
- I also teach students how to make dream catchers with branches. This includes a field trip near the school to collect the cedar branches. During the field trip I ask students to identify the different trees by looking at the branches and the cones that are on the ground. After our field trip I teach the students how to make a dream catcher using branches from trees. The students learn how to tie the string and weave inside the dream catcher.
- I invite my sister, Isabelle (Hill) Lewis to teach the students how to count from one to ten in the Smalgyax language. She teaches the students and reinforces the correct pronunciation by playing a game called "Around the world." I also teach the students how to count from one to ten in the French and the Haida language. This provides the students an opportunity to compare three different languages.
- I teach students the word *symmetry*. I ask questions about symmetry and how important symmetry is to the First Nations people. Provide the students with examples of First Nations drawings that contain half of a design. I use the butterfly to explain one example of symmetry.
- I have taught my grade two, three, and four classes at Seal Cove how to weave cedar roses, mats, and baskets. This was indeed a challenging project and I had my daughter

Stolly come in to assist me to teach my class how to make cedar roses. The students were beaming with pride and joy when they learned how to make a cedar rose for their Mother's Day gift. I also taught the students the process of how to get the bark off the trees and to understand the difference between the red and yellow cedar.

- Leah Robinson and I were team teachers. We taught the Tsimstiam "Respect" curriculum to grade five and six classes. This resource is great for teaching students how to respect themselves and others. We made a great team because we had different teaching styles and perspectives.
- I play the "listening game" with the students. The students sit around in a circle. The major concept of the game is to be able to listen to one complete sentence about a specific topic focused on First Nations culture. I whisper a sentence to them about information on various crests, what types of First Nations food I like to eat, or I provide examples of how to be respectful. The students pass the message on and when the sentence or information is passed around the circle correct, I tell them they are good listeners. A similar concept is using a feather or stone to pass around the circle. Students may share their feelings or a story. Only the person who is holding the object may talk, while the other students learn to listen.

I have been teaching at Roosevelt Elementary School for the last two years (2008-2010). This is an awesome school with strong leadership, great teachers, childcare workers, and friendly staff. It is a pleasant welcoming atmosphere where I enjoy teaching everyday. My gratitude and appreciation is expressed and acknowledged to Ms. Donalda Basso who has worked with me during these past few years. She has a heart of gold and we both work as a team to present the core components of the academic curriculum and First Nations Curriculum. Hopefully these examples of activities and strategies will be useful for teachers to use in a First Nations Studies unit.

Weaving

Since time immemorial our great ancestors have held the trees in the highest respect. The trees have given us their roots, branches, bark, and wood. Our ancestors used the cedar bark to weave clothing, diapers, regalia, cooking baskets, blankets, and mats. They also weaved baby cradles, dip nets, and ropes to raise totem poles. They also used the cedar to insulate longhouses and to make medicine. When I take the cedar, I say a prayer to thank the creator for giving me the lovely red and yellow cedar tree of life. When I weave, I feel a sense of peace and calmness. It is like a tranquil therapy. I love to weave. I can weave all day and I never get tired of weaving. When I sing Haida songs, I sing from my heart and soul. When I weave, I weave with this same energy and spirit. I weave from my heart and soul.

I remember watching my grandmother weave most of my life, but I never learned how to weave. It was my duty to listen and learn all our stories and history. I remember she told me how she dyed the bark red by using the red alder. She dyed the cedar black by burying the cedar in swamps behind the old church. She buried the cedar for a specific amount of time. If she left it in the swampy mud too long, the cedar turned mouldy. *Nonny* told me the Haida people believe that if they take all the cedar off the tree, the spirits of the cedar tree will not give them any more cedar. They also believe that a pregnant woman cannot weave or collect cedar bark when she is pregnant. They believed that the umbilical cord will wrap around the baby if they touch the cedar. The Haida people also used the cedar branches to cleanse themselves. It was used for medicine when a person had back pains. They used the cedar branches to rub or hit their back to heal their backaches. They used the bark, roots, and branches for many different medicinal uses.

In the days of my great grandmother, they used to teach the children how to weave when they were very young. They perfected their skills and they were taught by their maternal aunts with encouragement and support from the matriarchs. My experience was quite the opposite to this. I learned how to weave at a later age, when I was teaching at Prince Rupert Senior Secondary School. Colleen Williams and Marie Oldfield were my first basket-weaving teachers. I attended a weaving class which was sponsored by the Urban Haida Society. I joined this weaving class and this is how I learned how to weave my first basket. Colleen taught me how to make my first basket. I used rows of two strand twining of yellow cedar bark between each plaited row of red cedar. When I finished this basket, I weaved a cover for the basket. It was a beautiful basket. I was so proud of my basket. It was absolutely the best basket, simply because I made it. I made a goal to learn how to weave; I set my mind to weave and I made my first weaved basket.

Marie taught me how to make my second basket. I invited Marie to my class when I was teaching First Nations Studies 11/12 at Prince Rupert Senior Secondary School. This was my second experience in making a basket. I used checkerboard weaving with weft strands crossing over and under the warp strands. This was an enjoyable project. The students were pleased with their accomplishments after they completed their basket.

I always remember I wanted a cedar hat all my life, but I never received one. Despite wanting one so badly, no one ever thought of giving me a cedar hat, so I challenged myself to learn how to weave one. I thought if no one wants to give me a hat, I'll learn how to make my own hat. One summer, I bought a hat mold from the Skidegate Longhouse gift shop. I put my hat mold in my living room and it was there for several months.

One day, I was sitting with my hat mold in front of me and I was determined to learn how to weave a hat. No one showed me how to start a hat. No one told me what to do. I just remembered watching my grandmother weave. This skill was instilled in my mind and I started weaving a hat. My husband, Art said, "We are all born with special gifts. We just have to work to improve our skills and talents."

I discovered my weaving skills late in my life, but I take great pride in my creativity. I am very proud of my accomplishments and my skills in weaving. When I first started weaving, I did not get my own cedar bark. I focused my energy on learning the basic skills of how to weave. My husband has been getting the yellow cedar bark for me. He still strips the yellow cedar for me. My brother Isaac White also strips red cedar bark for me. Now, I have learned how to collect and pull my own red cedar bark. I enjoy going to strip the cedar from our homelands on Haida Gwaii.

My children and I go home to Haida Gwaii every summer to collect the red cedar. I select a tall slender tree with few branches and I say a prayer and thank the tree of life for giving me the beautiful cedar. This is the prayer I composed (In our language, *Howa* means thank you):

> *Howa* dear precious cedar trees,
> For giving me so freely of your beautiful cedar bark.
> *Howa* for your healing powers,
> For giving me roots and branches for medicine.
> *Howa* for your spiritual powers,
> I will take what I need and leave enough for continual growth.
> *Howa* for the beautiful gift of the cedar trees.

When we first started collecting red cedar at Massett, my son Tatzen, Jonus Penna, and my sister Adeline Penna were helping me get the red cedar bark. I use a small axe to cut and mark the tree in a horizontal cut. I cut in a straight angle up on both sides so I can pull the bark with a good grip using gloves to grab onto the cedar strips. For longer strips, I tie a rope around the bark to pull the red cedar. When the strips are falling off the tree, we have to be cautious while we are standing under the tree. Sometimes you have to move really fast when the long strips fall from the tree. We taught my son Tatzen and Jonus how to pull the bark off. They were eager and keen learners and their faces were shining with pride when they learned how to pull the bark off the trees.

They soon took over the duties to pull the bark off the trees, while Aunty Penna and I cleaned the outer bark off the red cedar. I cleaned the outer bark immediately and I start splitting the red cedar right away. It was a lot of work, but I wanted to experiment and work on the inner bark while the sap was wet. I usually pull three to four strips off one tree. It depends on the size of the tree. I use a small sharp knife to separate the outer bark from the inner bark. When the bark is too thick, I bend and break the outer bark off with my hands and knees. I like to clean the bark right away and roll the bark into a round coil immediately. Some weavers prefer to clean the inner bark when they are ready to weave. I prefer to clean the bark immediately. When I coil the cedar, I use cedar withes to tie up the cedar and pack the shining "red gold" onto my truck. I dry my cedar immediately either on a clothesline or in my basement for three to four days. When it is dry, I fold the cedar into round coils and tie it up with cedar withes and store it in paper boxes.

Yellow cedar is harder to find then the red cedar. The yellow cedar is strong and superior in quality. My husband pulls the yellow cedar in the month of July and August. It's absolutely amazing when I work with yellow cedar. It splits so fine and feels so silky when I am splitting the bark into strips. Sometimes I could split one length of bark into three layers. I start on the thick side to split the yellow bark. When I am splitting the cedar into strips, I can feel the bark in my hands and I know when the bark is getting too thin. I pull the bark in the opposite direction so the bark will even out. I love to smell the strong aroma of yellow cedar and the soft scent of red cedar when I am preparing the cedar to weave hats and baskets. I use the yellow cedar for rows of twining in between the plaiting of red cedar. When the yellow cedar is really pitchy, I use baby oil or butter so I can handle the cedar without the pitch sticking to my hands.

The methods differ for drying the red and yellow cedar. Some weavers prefer to sun dry or wind dry the cedar. The bark is soaked for several days and it can also be soaked in the river water or rain water. When it is soaked in the river water the bark turns a dark brown colour. Each weaver has different soaking methods depending on when they will clean the cedar to weave. I have experimented and used a variety of soaking methods.

I love to weave and I have accomplished my dream to weave hats, roses, vases, baskets, and weave on lighters. I weave around salt and pepper shakers and huge flower vases, and I weave tiny basket earrings. I also learned how to weave dream catchers and I used my creative skills to weave a mini longhouse.

My next challenge is to weave diagonally plaited baskets and use four cedar bark strands using horizontal strands and cross strands. I want to paint elegant designs on my hats and create more intricate designs and patterns on hats and baskets. I taught my daughter how to weave baskets, so she can carry on this wonderful art of weaving. She will pass this skill of weaving to her children, so the artistic knowledge of weaving will carry on forever.

Man in the Moon Design

The Haida Chief Who Build an Island

The oral traditions of the Haida people are stories of power. Each story has a moral, a lesson to teach, a link to our identity and our history. This story is about a Haida Chief who loved a princess so much he built an Island. This story is about values of compassion and love. Chief Guulaas is a Hereditary Chief from our clan, the Tsath Lanas Eagle Clan. My late grandmother told me this story years ago. There are many other versions of this story. I have rewritten this story to use in readers' theatre or an acting performance.

Characters:

Male Storyteller
Tsimpsian Chief
Haida Matriarch
Kitkatla Chief
Chief *Guulaas*
Kitkatla Princess
Four drummers
Four rattlers
Raven
Female Storyteller
Eagle
Haida Elder
Killer Whale
Nisga'a Chief

Drummers: Beat the drums in the same rhythm quietly. Boom – boom – boom. Every time the storytellers speak, the drummers quietly beat the drums in the background.

Rattles: Shake the rattles softly every time the storytellers speak. Quietly shake the rattles in the background.

Female Storyteller: Once upon a time, long before your time, long before my time, there was a brave Haida Chief who travelled all over the lands of Haida Gwaii. He travelled across the Hecate Strait and he travelled to Japan on huge canoes. He travelled all over the mainland, along the Northwest Coast of British Columbia.

Chief *Guulaas*: I have travelled all over the lands of Haida Gwaii. I have travelled to the Bering Straits, and I have travelled to Vancouver Island.

Male Storyteller: One day he travelled to the lands of the Tsimshian people on the mainland. He travelled to a place called Kitkatla Village. This was a time when the Haida people and the Kitkatla people were friendly. They were at peace. They were not at war. The great Chief welcomed Chief *Guulaas* onto his land.

***Chief Guulaas*:** It is time for me to travel to the land of the Kitkatla people.

Haida Matriarch: I will pray that you will have a safe journey.

Female Storyteller: The great Chief welcomed the Haida Chief onto his land. They went down to the beach to welcome the Chief.

Kitkatla Chief: Welcome to my territory. You are invited to come onto my land.

Chief *Guulaas*: I am a Chief from Haida Gwaii. My name is Chief *Guulaas*. We will row our canoes in backwards. This is the sign of peace for our people. *Howa*. Thank you for allowing us on your land.

Male Storyteller: It was known throughout the lands and Nations of the Haida and Nisga'a people that the Kitkatla Chief had a very beautiful daughter. She was renowned to all the people and she was well known in different villages near and far. She was known to be an elegant lady. She was also known to have a kind heart. Her fame spread throughout all the lands of the Haida Nation and up the Nass Valley.

Kitkatla Chief: Come to my village and we will have a big feast. My people will feed you and your clan members. Come to my longhouse and be my guest.

Chief *Guulaas*: We are honored to be your guest.

Kitkatla Chief: Come sit down and enjoy the food my family has prepared for you.

Chief *Guulaas*: Thank you for your kindness and thank you for all the food.

Kitkatla Chief: I am delighted to introduce you to my lovely daughter.

Chief *Guulaas*: It is an honor to meet your beautiful daughter.

Kitkatla Princess: Welcome to my father's territory.

Female Storyteller: Many great Chiefs from all the different Nations came to the land of the Kitkatla people. Each Chief wanted to marry the lovely princess. One Chief brought the Kitkatla Chief many gifts of copper. Many Chiefs from all over the mainland came with great wealth to give to the Kitkatla Chief and asked to marry the princess.

Nisga'a Chief: Chief of Kitkatla Village, I have brought you many great gifts. I have come to ask you to marry your beautiful daughter.

Kitkatla Chief: I cannot accept your gifts. I love my daughter and I do not want her to leave this village.

Tsimshian Chief: I have brought you gifts of copper and gold. I truly admire your beautiful daughter. I have come to ask your permission to marry your daughter.

Kitkatla Chief: My wife and I do not want our daughter to leave our village. I cannot accept your gifts.

Male Storyteller: The Kitkatla Chief and his wife loved their daughter and they were cautious and selective in choosing her husband. The Haida Chief travelled back to his territory on Haida Gwaii. After many days he travelled back to Kitkatla on his huge canoes. He came with an abundance of wealth to give to the Kitkatla Chief. The Haida Chief met the beautiful Princess and he fell in love with her but the Chief refused to give her hand in marriage to any Chief.

Chief *Guulaas*: I have brought you many gifts in our huge canoes. I have brought you carved totem poles and copper shields.

Kitkatla Chief: I have turned away many great Chiefs from the Nisga'a Nation and Tsimshian Nation. My wife and I love our daughter. We are very careful in choosing the right man to marry her.

Chief *Guulaas*: I have brought you magnificent carvings. The totem poles are carved out of argillite. We are the only people who carve out of this beautiful black stone.

Kitkatla Chief: Thank you for your gifts of wealth, but I do not want my daughter to live far away from our people.

Female Storyteller: Chief *Guulaas* travelled back to Haida Gwaii with sadness in his heart. He loved the princess and he decided to go back to give more gifts to the Kitkatla Chief. When he arrived in the land of the Kitkatla people, he went to the Kitkatla Chief. He asked him to marry his beautiful daughter again. The Kitkatla Chief told the Haida Chief he will consider his request.

Chief *Guulaas*: I have come back to ask you to marry your daughter again. I have brought more elegant gifts. I have brought you masks, copper shields, and huge magnificent cedar totem poles.

Kitkatla Chief: Thank you for your beautiful gifts. You have come back again to ask to marry my daughter. I believe you love my daughter. I will consider your request.

Male Storyteller: It was many days before the Kitkatla Chief called the Haida Chief back to his longhouse. He invited him to eat *oolican* grease with smoked seal meat, boiled potatoes, seaweed, smoked *oolicans,* and soap berries. He told the Chief he did not want his daughter to leave his village. Haida Gwaii is too far away. The Kitkatla Chief told the Haida Chief to build an Island near his village and he will give the Haida Chief permission to marry his daughter.

Kitkatla Chief: Go to call the Haida Chief to come to my longhouse.

Chief *Guulaas*: I have come to your longhouse. I am honored to be your guest.

Kitkatla Chief: I called you to come and eat with my family. I want to tell you that we love our daughter. We do not want her to leave our village.

Chief *Guulaas*: I love your daughter and I will do anything you ask me to do.

Kitkatla Chief: I have thought about how we can keep our daughter nearby our village. I want you to build me an Island nearby and then I will give you permission to marry my daughter.

Chief *Guulaas*: Thank you great Chief. I will fulfil your wish. I will build you an Island.

Female Storyteller: Chief *Guulaas* travelled back to his village. He met with all the Elders and matriarchs of his clan. They all knew he loved the princess. They wanted to help him build an Island, but they could not think of how to build this Island for the Kitkatla Chief.

Chief *Guulaas*: Go and call all the Elders and matriarchs. I am calling a big gathering. We will find out how to build an Island for the Kitkatla Chief.

Haida Matriarch: Great Chief, we have come here to help you. We know that you love the beautiful princess. We will help you to build an Island.

Male Storyteller: The Haida Chief went to bed and he could not think of how to build an Island. He soon became disheartened because he could not find an answer.

Haida Elder: Dear Chief, we have thought about your request. We cannot think of how you can build this Island.

Chief *Guulaas*: I feel very discouraged. I love the princess and I will find a way to build the Island for the Kitkatla Chief.

Female Storyteller: Chief *Guulaas* went to bed and he had a dream of how to build the Island. In his dream he saw all the birds and sea animals. The next day he woke up with great happiness. He gathered all the Elders, advisors, and matriarchs together to tell everyone about his plan.

Chief *Guulaas*: I want all the Elders and matriarchs to come to my longhouse immediately.

Haida Matriarch: What is your plan? How are you going to build an Island?

Chief *Guulaas*: The answer was given to me in my dreams. I dreamed about how the birds and sea animals can help me build an Island.

Haida Elder: How will the birds and sea animals help you?

Chief *Guulaas*: I will ask all the birds and sea animals to help me bring stones and pebbles, leaves and grass and drop them into the water.

Haida Matriarch: It is our tradition to feed all the people and animals when you ask them for help. We must feed all the birds and sea animals.

Chief *Guulaas*: Give this message to all our people. We must gather all kinds of food so we can feed the birds and sea animals.

Male Storyteller: The Haida Chief called the raven, eagle, and killer whale. He asked them to be his messengers to go ask all the birds and sea animals to help him build an Island. The Island will be built on Kitkatla territory. Chief *Guulaas* told the birds and sea animals that his clan members will feed them everyday for their generous help.

Chief *Guulaas*: Come to me raven. Come to me eagle. Come to me killer whale. I am asking you to be my messengers. It is your duty to go to all the birds and sea animals to ask them to help me build an Island.

Raven: I will go and fly all over the Islands of Haida Gwaii and ask all the ravens and birds to come help you build an Island.

Eagle: I will be honored to help you build an Island. I will fly all over the lands and oceans to give the message to all the birds and sea animals to come help you.

Killer Whale: I will travel far and wide in the oceans, rivers, inlets, and streams to tell all the sea animals to come and help you.

Female Storyteller: While the eagle, raven, and killer whale went to spread this message around the lands on Haida

Gwaii, all the people in his eagle clan were gathering food for months. They gathered enough food to feed the birds and sea animals every day.

Haida Matriarch: We have gathered clams, seaweed, cockles, and berries.

Haida Elder: The young men have gathered deer meat and fresh water.

Haida Matriarch: Our people have gathered enough food to feed thousands of birds and sea animals.

Male Storyteller: Then all the eagles, ravens, hummingbirds, sparrows, owls, seagulls, and every bird came flying to help build the Island. Soon all the grey whales, salmon, trout, sockeye, sea otters, killer whales, and all the sea animals came to help build an Island. He told the birds and sea animals that he has to build an Island and the Kitkatla Chief will give him permission to marry the princess. He asked them for their help. The Haida Chief was grateful they all came to help him.

Raven: The hummingbirds, blue jays, seagulls, and robins have come to help you build an Island.

Eagle: The crows, geese, and birds will help you. The owls and ravens have come to help you too.

Killer Whale: The trout, sockeye, crabs, and sea otters have come to help and the sea animals will continue to tell all the other sea creatures to come and help build the Island.

Female Storyteller: The next day there were thousands of birds in the air. In the ocean and inlets there were thousands of sea animals that came to help Chief *Guulaas.* The Chief was very pleased and honored they came to help him. He decided to travel back to Kitkatla. He took hundreds of canoes filled with food to feed the birds and sea animals.

Chief *Guulaas*: *How-a.* Thank you. I am honored. I will accept your help.

Haida Matriarch: The men will load up all the canoes with food and water.

Chief *Guulaas*: We will travel to Kitkatla immediately.

Haida Elder: Our Elders will pray that you will have a safe journey. We will pray the birds and sea animals will build a beautiful Island that will satisfy the Kitkatla Chief.

Male Storyteller: When they arrived in the land of the Kitkatla people, they started to build the Island near Kitkatla Village. Each bird took small stones in their beak and carried the stones to drop into the water. The sea animals took gravel, stones and weeds. This work continued for many months. The Haida Chief and his clan fed the birds and sea animals every day. During the night the owls continued to carry stones and pebbles. It took many months before the sea was covered and they could finally see the gravel and the beginning of a new Island.

Raven: All the raccoons, porcupines, bears, deer, and sparrows are working every day. The owls are working hard every night.

Killer whale: All the crabs, whales, jelly fish, eels, trout, and seals are bringing many weeds and pebbles to help build the Island.

Eagle: Thank you for feeding us every day.

Female Storyteller: Chief *Guulaas* was delighted and proud of the birds' and sea animals' efforts in helping him build an Island. He fed them every day and they continued to bring gravel. They continued to bring leaves, grass and branches. Soon the flowers and grass started to grow. Soon the cedar trees and the bushes started to grow.

Chief *Guulaas*: *Howa.* Thank you. I am grateful for all your hard work.

Haida Elder: The birds and sea animals are making a great Island. The grass is starting to grow and the flowers are growing.

Male Storyteller: It was time to go to the Kitkatla Chief. The Chief did not know Chief *Guulaas* was building this magnificent Island. The Haida Chief gathered all the birds and sea animals for a big potlatch. He thanked them for their kindness and all the work they did to help build the Island.

Haida Matriarch: It is time to put on a huge potlatch to thank all the birds and sea animals.

Chief *Guulaas*: All my precious Haida people. I want to thank all the generous birds and sea animals. I am grateful for all the work you did for me. You have built a strikingly beautiful Island. It is time for me to go to the Kitkatla Chief. I will take him to see the Island and I will ask him to marry his fine-looking daughter.

Female Storyteller: The Haida Chief went to the Kitkatla Chief and told him he has built an Island. He asked the Chief to marry his daughter. The Chief could not believe he built an Island. Chief *Guulaas* told him that he asked the Creator to help him and he sent all the birds and sea animals to help him.

Chief *Guulaas*: I have come to ask you to marry your daughter. I have fulfilled your wish. I have built you an Island.

Kitkatla Chief: Take me to see this Island.

Chief *Guulaas*: The Island is built near your village.

Kitkatla Chief: You are an admirable Chief. You have my permission to marry my daughter.

Chief *Guulaas*: I will be honored to marry your daughter. I will protect her and I will love her from now to eternity.

Kitkatla Princess: Thank you my dear father. I love the Haida Chief and I will be proud to marry him.

Male Storyteller: The Kitkatla Chief was happy that his daughter would not go far away from her homeland. He gave permission to Chief *Guulaas* to marry his attractive daughter. The Haida Chief and the princess lived on the Island near the land of the Kitkatla people and they lived a long and happy life.

Tow and Tow-Ustahsin

Nonny told me this story when I was a young girl. There are many versions of this story. I have rewritten this story for children to use in readers theatre or to act in a drama play. This is a wonderful story and it teaches children different lessons and morals.

Characters:
Storyteller
Tow
Tow-Ustahsin
Chief of the Sea
Chorus

Storyteller: A long time ago there were twin brothers who lived on Haida Gwaii. Their names are Tow and Tow-Ustahsin. They were born at a place called *Juskatla* Inlet. When the brothers were young they lived a happy life at *Juskatla* Inlet for many years.

Tow: We are very fortunate. We have a good life.

Tow-Ustahsin: Yes brother. We have been very happy here.

Tow: We have plenty of food. There is lots of salmon here for us to eat.

Tow-Ustahsin: There is sockeye, deer meat, and lots of food here.

Storyteller: Soon the two brothers grew older. Every person has different types of character. The twin brothers have their own personality and behavior. Tow was a kind young man. He has a warm heart and he has love and respect for all the animals and nature. Tow-Ustahsin was not like his brother. He had an ill temper and he would complain and get upset over everything. He became irritated when he did not get his own way.

Tow: Brother, you must learn to be patient.

Tow-Ustahsin: I don't have to listen to you.

Tow: When someone treats you nice, you should learn to be nice too.

Tow-Ustahsin: I can do whatever I want to do. I don't have to listen to you.

Storyteller: There is always a great quantity of salmon in the Inlet. The Chief of the Sea was very generous and always gave salmon and halibut to the brothers.

Chief of the Sea: I have brought you gifts of halibut and clams.

Tow-Ustahsin: My brother is not here to eat the halibut.

Chief of the Sea: I bring gifts of food for both of you.

Tow-Ustahsin: You can give me the halibut and clams you brought for my brother. I will eat his share.

Chief of the Sea: No. I will not give you his share of food.

Tow-Ustahsin: I can eat all the food. Tow is not here. I will eat all the seafood.

Storyteller: Tow was upset with his brother's behavior. He listened to his brother complain all the time. He listened to his constant nagging. Tow was getting tired of his negative attitude. One day when he went to sleep, his brother Tow-Ustahsin decided he would do something to his brother Tow. There was a huge run of salmon that afternoon while his brother was sleeping. Tow-Ustahsin thought he would give his brother something to talk about, so he went and ate up all the salmon.

Tow: Brother, I am going to take a nap in the warm sun.

Tow-Ustahsin: Yes brother. Go take a nap.

Storyteller: When Tow woke up from his nap he became very upset when he discovered his brother ate up all the salmon.

Tow: Why did you eat up all the food?

Tow-Ustahsin: I ate up all the salmon so you could have something to complain about.

Tow: I am your brother. You should learn how to share with your family.

Storyteller: Tow was angry. He was furious. He would not allow his brother to treat him this way again. He decided to leave *Juskatla* Inlet forever. He left that evening when the moon was full and the evening was bright. He left with great anger and rage. He went storming down the Inlet. All the people were terrified by the noise Tow was making.

Tow: I will leave this place forever. My brother does not treat me right.

Chorus: Boom – boom – boom (action: stomp your feet)

Storyteller: When Tow reached the village of Massett, the moon was slowly becoming dim. The night became dark. Tow could not travel across the Hecate Strait. He went half way across the channel and he could not see. He was forced to go back. He became angry and he stomped around so much, he made the place known today as *Delkatla* Slough. He changed direction and he travelled to a place called *Chown* Point. While he was stomping to his new destination, he left behind huge rocks. These rocks are still seen to this day.

Tow: I will travel across the channel. I will find a new home.

Chorus: Boom – boom – boom (action: stomp your feet).

Tow: I cannot go across the channel. It's too dark. I will go back to Haida Gwaii.

Storyteller: Tow rested at *Chown* Point and he stayed there for several months. He did not like it there because there was not enough salmon. He decided to leave. Tow stomped his way to *Yakan* Point. While he was stomping his way he left behind many big rocks.

Tow: I will rest at *Chown* Point for a while. After I rest, I will leave because there is not enough food here.

Chorus: Boom – boom – boom (action: stomp your feet).

Storyteller: Tow liked it at *Yakan* Point. There was lots of salmon and he could have all the food he wanted in this area. There are clams, sea urchins, and crabs. No one will steal his food and he decided to stay. He looked around for a good site where it would be suitable for a hill of his size. He found a place at the bank of *Hiellen* River and he decided he would remain there forever.

Tow: I like this area. There is plenty of salmon and plenty of seafood here. I will make my home here. I will live here forever where everyone can admire me.

Storyteller: Tow enjoyed living near the sandy beach. Now there is peace and harmony in their family. His brother enjoyed living at *Juskatla* and Tow-Ustahsin still remains there to this day. Tow still remains at *Hiellen* River. Everyone who goes to Haida Gwaii will go to admire him as a hill called *Tow* Hill.

The Raven and the Moon

Characters:
Raven
Jaaboo
Baajoo

Storyteller: Many years ago the Raven was flying around the shores of *Tow* Hill. He flew along the sandy beach and then the Raven flew around Massett Inlet. One day the Raven saw two Haida men fishing on their canoe.

Raven: Please give me a salmon. I am very hungry.

Jaaboo: I will give you one piece of our sockeye.

Raven: Thank you for your kindness.

Storyteller: The Raven followed the fishermen everyday. He circled around their canoe and he would ask for salmon.

Raven: I am hungry. Can you give me one piece of sockeye?

Baajoo: Here is one sockeye.

Storyteller: The fishermen were very generous. Soon the Raven became very lazy. Instead of hunting for his own food, he proceeds to fly around the Haida men and begged for more food. Soon they became very tired of feeding the Raven. They stopped giving the Raven food. Everyday the Raven went flying above the men waiting for a chance to swoop down and steal the salmon.

Raven: The Haida men will not give me any more food. I will steal the biggest sockeye from their fishing nets.

Jaaboo: We will not feed you anymore. You cannot steal from us. We fed you too long. You are a greedy Raven. You must find your own food.

Storyteller: The Raven became very angry and the Raven circled around the men's canoe and yelled threats at the fishermen. The fishermen became tired of the Raven. They started throwing stones at the Raven to stop the Raven from yelling threats.

Baajoo: Stop bothering us.

Raven: If you don't give me anymore salmon. I will get my revenge on you. Next sockeye season you will see what I will do.

Storyteller: The Haida men were concerned about what the Raven would do because they depended on the sockeye every season. As time passed they forgot about the Raven's threats.

Jaaboo: The Raven cannot hurt us.

Storyteller: The days went by and soon a year passed and it was time for the men to go out fishing for sockeye. When they were out fishing they soon heard the Raven's voice.

Raven: I have come back for my revenge. When the moon comes out, you will find out what I am going to do.

Baajoo: I wonder what the Raven is going to do!

Storyteller: Soon it became dark and the moon was shining bright across the water. The Haida men stayed in their canoes and soon the moon began to rise high in the sky above.

Jaaboo: We should not be afraid of the threats from the Raven.

Baajoo: Let's keep fishing for more sockeye.

Storyteller: When the moon was shining high, the Raven came flying over to the Haida men. The Raven began circling around their canoe.

Raven: I am going to steal the moon and you will not be able to catch any more sockeye.

Jaaboo: No one can steal the moon. It is too high in the sky.

Baajoo: Ha! Ha! You cannot steal the moon.

Storyteller: When the Haida fishermen started laughing at the Raven, he became very angry. He flew high in the air to the moon and snatched the moon in his beak and he started flying far away from the men. Soon it began to get darker and darker.

Jaaboo: Please come back with the moon. We will not laugh at you again.

Baajoo: We are sorry we laughed at you. Come back with the moon.

Jaaboo: We will carve you on our totem poles and all our carvings. Please bring back the moon. We cannot see. We cannot catch any more salmon.

Raven: I will bring back the moon if you promise to carve me on all your totem poles and you must give me sockeye when I am hungry.

***Baajoo*:** We promise to carve the Raven on all our totem poles, house fronts and crest designs, and on all our wood carvings.

Storyteller: The Raven brought back the moon and to this day the moon continues to shine on the lands of Haida Gwaii. The Haida people kept their promise to carve the Raven on all their carvings and totem poles.

Raven and Woman Design

Traditions and Culture

In Indian tradition each adult is personally responsible for each child, to see that he learns all he needs to know in order to live a good life. As our fathers had a clear idea of what made a good man and a good life in their society, so we modern Indians want our children to learn that happiness and satisfaction come from: pride in one's self, understanding one's fellow men and living in harmony with nature.
National Indian Brotherhood, 1972

The Haida people have two major symbols of identity called the eagle and raven moiety. The crests are a symbol of identity and integral to the social system. Today we have a social insurance number or a driver's license that identify who we are in this society. Our crests are a symbol of our identity which is passed down from generation to generation. The crests are like an identification card that indicates our family identity. The crest is a symbol of our family history and represents a sense of belonging. Crests are carved on totem poles to explain our history. Each crest signifies membership in a hereditary identity that is passed on through our mother's lineage.

The crests are powerful symbols which represents each clan's identity. Each clan has several crests. For example, the *Tsath Lanas* clan has seven crests. The first crest is called the double headed eagle. This crest came from *Nonny* Amanda's great uncle. He married a woman from Alaska and he lived there for the remainder of his life. When his wife died, he felt very sad. He went to sit down on the beach and he saw an eagle sitting on a tree stump. The eagle kept moving its head from side to side. It looked like it had two heads. This is when our great-great uncle took this crest for our clan. Our great uncles also travelled to Victoria B.C. by canoe. During those days, they saw all the beautiful flowers so they took the flowers called Forget-me-not as our crest.

For every crest a clan has a story to signify how they received a specific crest. The other crests we have in our clan are the grey whale, frog, blackfish, and bear.

It is important to identify how many fins each killer whale has to clarify which crests belong to each clan. Our crest called the grey whale has one fin. The other eagle clans have two fins, three fins, four fins and up to five fins. The other crest we have is the elegant frog. The frog is significance of healing and the frog gives us strength. The bear crest is our spiritual healer.

The Haida people have many crests. The different types of crests are humming bird, grizzly bear, killer whale, thunder-bird, skate, cumulus clouds, grey whale, five finned killer whale, frog, wolf as well as many other different animal figures or supernatural symbols.

This is a story about when a bear was trapped at Naden Harbour on *Tsath Lanas* territory. Our great ancestors are also known as the Up Inlet people. Long before my great great grandmother's time, a bear was trapped near Kung. The young *Tsath Lanas* eagle warriors made a trap for the bear. The woman made long strong ropes out of red and yellow cedar. They used strong woven cedar ropes and cedar trees to make a huge trap. The men dug a gigantic hole and covered the hole with moss and cedar branches. Then they waited patiently for several days and soon the bear was trapped. The warriors raised the bear from the deep hole and they cut the fur. During the night a *Tsath Lanas* warrior put on the skin and the bear told the warrior to learn to respect the bear people. He said, "Do not be afraid. Do not fear me. I will provide you with bear's bread to use as medicine." The bears can sense when humans are afraid of them. The bear is the protector and healer. This is how the *Tsath Lanas* clan took the bear for their crest. This is an old story told several generations ago. To this day, we still use the bear's bread as a strong, powerful medicine. We use the medicine for stress, stroke, and to protect our families.

Each clan has their own stories about how they received their crest symbols. When other people see our clan wearing these symbols, they know which clan we come from. These crests are a symbol of our identity.

The Haida people use many different herbs, plants, and trees for medicines. *Nonny* showed me all kinds of medicine. One example is the pitch from the trees. I remember when I was eleven years old. My cousins and I were playing down by the beach. I fell down and skinned my knee. I went to *Nonny's* house and she immediately boiled spruce pitch to use for medicine to put on my knee. She used a piece of red cedar bark to put the hot pitch on my knee. I remember that I was scared because I could see the pitch steaming in a pot on top of the wood stove. *Nonny* said, "Don't worry, it will sting for a while but this will make your knee heal." *Nonny* put the pitch on my knee, it stung and the pitch was steaming hot. A few days later the pitch healed my knee and there was no scar.

The Haida people use various herbs to boil and drink as tea. I remember when we were young kids, *Nonny* always sent us behind the church to pick yellow skunk cabbage. The Elders use the skunk cabbage roots for coughs and asthma. The roots is also dried and used in specific amounts to drink for bad coughs. The leaves are crushed and dried to drink for headaches. The men were responsible to get the lily roots. The elders use the water lily leaves and roots for boils and swelling. We had to drive to *Tlell* or the roads to *Juskatla* to pick pussy willows. The Elders used the pussy willows and stinging nettles for headaches. Sometimes the stinging nettles are used when a pregnant woman is overdue. We ask the opposite clan to pick the stinging nettles when it is used for other purposes. When the stinging nettle is in season, I use the traditional method to get the stinging nettles. I ask the opposite clan member to get the stinging nettles. My niece is from the Raven clan; I asked

Kathleen White to pick the stinging nettles for me. It is our tradition to pay the opposite clan when we ask them to do something for us. All the herbs and medicines grow on Haida Gwaii. Each medicine must be picked during the right season. I was very fortunate to have *Nonny* teach me how to make various medicines. These are only a few of the herbs and plants we use for medicinal uses. I'm always amazed at how brilliant our ancestors were to utilize all the herbs and cedar for medicinal uses.

In our culture names are very important. Names are one of the most important means of social organization for the Haida people. In the olden days, the names were a great significance of wealth and power. The names make you responsible, and each person regardless of status or rank must earn their names. Our ancestors gave names to longhouses, canoes, and land. Each name is considered lineage property. It is forbidden to take another clan's name. However, it is known that a name can be "borrowed" from another clan. When the name is borrowed from another clan, this is made known in a public potlatch. When the person who borrowed the name has received their own name from their clan, then the name they borrowed is given back to the rightful owner or clan. The person who borrowed the name must give a gift to the rightful owner and thank them for using the Haida name. This is done in an honorable fashion and acknowledged at a potlatch.

Today we receive a name at a potlatch. All the names are validated and witnessed in a feast or potlatch. The names are our identity. We bestow a name to a clan member anytime during a clan feast or potlatch. The Elders make sure the names are transferred to their grandchildren to ensure continuity of our lineage. The names are very special and unique. In the *Tsath Lanas* clan we give four clan members the same name. For example; my great grandmother's name was Kaakuns. Her English name was Kate Bell. This name was passed down to my mother and Rosie Brown. In the year 2006, I had the honour to have the name Kaakuns bestowed to me. I have two Haida names. Oolonkuthway and Kaakuns. Oolonkuthway means Shining Gold and Kaakuns means "story keeper or storyteller." This is indeed an appropriate name for me because I know our history and I am a storyteller. The reason why we give four people the same name is to carry on the family names and lineage. The Haida names are immortal because we carry on our names and pass them on to each generation forever.

There are many different types of adoptions. These are examples of how we adopt a person. Many years ago, I was adopted by Mamie Jones. She has five daughters named; Erma Gagnon, Mavis Delill, Adeline Penna, Rose Bell, and Jane Mennie. When my only sister Stolly died, Mamie Jones told me she was going to adopt me. Several years later she adopted me and she said, "You will never be alone. I will give you five of my daughters to be your sister." Adeline, Mavis, and Rose have always been my best friends and now they are my sisters.

Another type of adoption is when Adam Bell adopted Art Collison into the Raven clan. He adopted him so he could marry a Haida woman from the Eagle clan. During the memorial headstone moving of the Late Minnie Edgars, the Hereditary Chief of our clan adopted three people. Ken Edgars adopted Rick Borne and Rick Grange as his brothers and he also adopted Jana McDonald as his sister. I had the honor of giving them Haida names. I named Jana "Smart Girl." Rick Borne's name is "Big Heart" and Rick Grange's name is "Strong Mind."

When we had the memorial totem pole raising for my grandmother, my mother adopted Isabelle (Hill) Lewis. This particular adoption took one year to arrange. My mother and members of our family travelled to Prince Rupert to meet Isabelle's family to get approval to adopt her into our family. Later she travelled over to Haida Gwaii to meet members of our family. When both families approved this adoption, my mother proceeded to adopt Isabelle during the memorial potlatch of my late grandmother. My mother named her Git Sim Haida Jud Kwiiaas. *Git* stems from *Gitsan, Sim* comes from Tsimshian. and *Jud Kwiiaas* means "precious sister." Isabelle

Lewis is my precious sister. My mother also adopted Kevin Lagroix, Jack Bucknell, and Leonard Watts. I also had the honor of giving Marilyn Bryant a Haida name. Rick, George, and Judy Williams are also my adopted family. They lived with us when they were young children. They call me "Big Sis." These are my adopted brothers and sisters.

The potlatch is part of the Haida social system. The word potlatch means "to give" or "to give things away." Food sharing is at the heart of every potlatch. This is witnessed by the guests who enjoyed the finest seafood, stew, homemade buns, and deserts. We give potlatches to commemorate occasions such as a headstone moving, a name giving, a marriage, a totem pole raising, a face saving feast, and naming a Hereditary Chief. People are invited to witness and validate a tradition or specific name giving. When the people accept the gifts as payment for witnessing an event, this validates our oral traditions, culture, and history. We had no written language; therefore, we verbalize the history. When we tell our history at a potlatch, the history is recorded and locked into the minds and hearts of the people who are witnessing the ceremony. Through oral traditions and oral history our ancestors recorded our history by telling stories, carving our history on totem poles, making family crests, and delivering speeches at potlatches and feasts. When the people accept the gifts, they acknowledge the rights and privileges owned by the Chief who gave the potlatch.

At the potlatch, each clan displays their crests and performs songs and dances. The potlatch is the most important ceremony for the Haida people. It is a time when we celebrate our cultural traditions of songs and dances. There are over seven dance groups in Massett. Often there is several dance groups from Massett and Skidegate who entertain and perform at every potlatch. All the Haida singers gather up in front of the community hall to sing songs and entertain the guests while they are eating. It is indeed a proud moment for me and for the community when the singers beat their drums and sing so powerful. It makes my heart swell with happiness to listen to the powerful voices of the Haida people who are singing at the potlatches. I'm not shy, so I always go up and sing with all the Haida singers when there is a potlatch at my home town, Old Massett.

We display a great sense of humor in the songs and dances. An example is when Adeline Penna and Uncle Dean Edgars were dancing to a song I sung at *Nonny's* Memorial potlatch. I sang a song called "Hey Good Looking." I started the song by singing "*hey hey hey*" and then changed the words into the English language. It was humorous and rather entertaining. I proceeded to sing the song louder and I sing some jazz into the rhythm. Adeline and Uncle Dean were wearing funny masks and they were dancing real jazzy for the audience. We made everyone laugh and we had so much fun. Laughter is indeed a good medicine. It cures the heart, mind, and soul.

The potlatches are also a time when we display community spirit and social warmth. It is a time when all the Haida people dress in their finest traditional regalia. Many of the men and women wear their beautiful cedar hats and elegantly designed shawls, dresses, and blazers. It is a time when we make a statement by dressing in our finest regalia to show people that we are proud to be a Haida. It is a time when we socialize and meet old friends or make new friends. It is a time when we join in the clan dances and sing Haida songs. At every potlatch, the host displays their hospitality and generosity by providing lots of food for all the people. At each potlatch, all the people are encouraged to take food home to remember the generosity of the clan that hosted the potlatch. In the Haida tradition we call this *gowkith*. It is considered an insult if a guest doesn't take any food home.

We follow protocol and show respect to the Elders. In each potlatch people are seated according to their importance. All the Hereditary Chiefs and their wives are seated on the head table in front of all the guests. The matriarchs and Elders are seated at the head table and each Elder is held in high esteem. In the days of our great ancestors the people were seated according to their rank. They were seated in order as follows: Hereditary Chief, nobles, medicine men, matriarchs, and Elders. In the potlatch, the Hereditary Chief of the territory gives the first speech, followed by the other Haida Hereditary Chiefs from Haida Gwaii, then the matriarchs, Elders, Council of Haida Nation President, and local Chief Counsellor. The Elders always give a speech in the Haida language. The Hereditary Chiefs tells where their traditional territories are located. They identify their crests and tell stories that have been passed down through each generation.

Today we still celebrate the following potlatches:

Hereditary Chief potlatch
Headstone Moving
Memorial Potlatch & Feast
Name Giving potlatch
Face Saving potlatch

The potlatches were banned in 1890 through the *Indian Act.* The potlatches that did not survive after the Federal Government banned the potlatches are the Vengeance potlatch. This is a potlatch given by a high ranking person who has been insulted.

The Puberty feast did not survive. This is a feast that is similar to a small dinner when there are invited guests that come to witness the completion of the girl's puberty. The mother and her family members give this feast when a girl completes her puberty seclusion. The other feasts called the perforation of ears, nose and lower lips, house dedication feasts, and competitive challenges are still held but very rarely. My grandmother and mother witnessed these types of feasts during their generation. Today the house dedication feasts are still held in our community.

One of the protocols to name a Chief is through the system of the Eldest son of the Eldest person in the clan. Since time immemorial the Haida people go under the matrilineal system, there lineage and identify is followed through their mother's side of the family. An example is when the mother is a white person the children go under their mother's side or when the mother is from another First Nations lineage (e.g. Nisga'a, Tsimshian, etc.), the children automatically follow the mother's lineage. In order to be acknowledged as a Matriarch, the woman held in high esteem are the oldest living women of each clan. The Matriarch for the *Tsath Lanas* clan is Martha Keisman (formerly White). She is the eldest living woman in our clan.

Sometimes the person in line to become a Hereditary Chief can be rejected by people within the clan. When the people turn their blankets inside out and demonstrate this in a public potlatch, the person who is becoming a Chief is not accepted. This is a powerful statement to demonstrate that the Haida people do not agree with the person who is becoming a Chief. Another form of rejection is a written statement signed by the Hereditary Chiefs. Sometimes people will simply refuse to attend the potlatch if they reject the Chief.

The face saving potlatch is still practiced today. An example of this type of potlatch is when a Haida man hit another Haida person or when a Haida man insults a Hereditary Chief. The person who caused injury or insult must put on a potlatch and bestow elegant, extravagant gifts to the person they insulted or injured. When the person accepts these gifts in a potlatch, the person is forgiven and they have regained their honor.

Today we still have feasts immediately after funerals to honor outstanding individuals or a loved one that has passed on. The feast is different from a potlatch. Some people chose to have a feast when a loved one dies. They provide tea, clam chowder or seafood stew, sandwiches, and desert for all the people after the funeral services. The people pay their respects to the loved one that passed away. Their presence at the feast gives comfort to the bereaved family. A memorial potlatch takes place one year after the death of a loved one. Sometimes the headstone potlatch takes longer than a year. The length of time depends on each family or clan. All the family members help to purchase gifts to be given away at the potlatch. During this type of potlatch, the family distributes gifts or money to the people who helped dig the grave, pallbearers, and the women who wiped the headstone. In the memorial potlatch, the Haida people have a tradition of paying the opposite clan for their kind service.

It is a tradition to pay the women who wipes the headstone. For example, our clan paid everyone who helped us when we had the headstone moving ceremonies for my late brother Herman, my late sister Stolly, and my late dad. Our family is from the eagle moiety; therefore, we paid the raven members who were pallbearers and the raven women who wiped the headstones. My dad is from the raven clan, so we paid a woman from the eagle clan to wipe his headstone. We paid the local Church Army and the Anglican Church. The Church Army group always visits the family's home to comfort the family who lost a loved one. They sing songs and pray for the bereaved family members. In the Village of Old Masset, the congregation is usually led by Marina Jones or Reverend Lily Bell. These are two wonderful, caring women who are always available to pray and support the Haida people. When we had our headstone moving potlatch for my brother, sister, and dad, we paid all the people for helping us during the loss of our loved ones. Each person who came to witness the potlatch received several gifts. We gave exceptional gifts to the Hereditary Chiefs and their wives.

At each potlatch, we celebrate the revival of cultural traditions, which range from serving sea foods, gift giving, displaying artwork, singing traditional songs, and performing various dances. The guests witness the validation of names, territories, and the special and unique way we honor the loss of loved ones and passing on Haida names. The guests witness a totem pole raising and the naming of a Hereditary Chief. They witness and validate the Haida culture.

Shark Woman Design

Basket Full of Stories

> *The Medicine Wheel or Drum has become a popular symbol for helping First Nations people articulate a definition of health. Intellectual; concepts, ideas, thoughts, habits, discipline. Spiritual; A sense of connectedness with other creations of the Great Spirit. Emotional; love, recognition, acceptance, understanding, privacy, limits, discipline. Physical; air, water, food, clothing, shelter, exercise, sex. The circle represents wholeness and movement or action. Having effective ways and means to satisfy fundamental physical and emotional needs, a person is able to focus energies upon creating knowledge or working tools which will equip him to define, redefine and pursue his purpose on this earth.*
>
> Mussell, Nicholls & Adler, 1991

My mind is filled with songs and stories. I want you to imagine all the stories are strips of cedar bark. All my stories are represented by the exquisite red and yellow cedar bark. I am weaving a cedar basket as a symbol that represents wholeness of learning the stories. The strips of cedar represent four major elements called physical, spiritual, emotional, and mental. I weave the bark together into a beautiful basket full of stories. These components are identified as follows:

Physical: body, behaviour, and hands.
Spiritual: values, beliefs, respect, and the Creator.
Emotional: feelings, heart, and love.
Mental: cognitive, intellectual, head, thinking, listening, and learning.

Physical relates to the body, behaviour, and hands. It includes the air, water, and food. It includes the exercise we need to keep our bodies healthy. It includes clothing, environment, and Mother Earth. The physical and protection symbol is the "helping hands," which signify how we help each other and how we use our hands to preserve foods, protect the land, and protect our families.

Spirituality encompasses our values, beliefs, and our Creator. We have spiritual needs for purpose, meaning, and a connection to nature and other creations. One of the first values is respect. *Nonny* said, "You have to learn to respect yourself before you will be able to respect others." The dimensions and concepts of respect relate to the land, nature, animals, and other people.

The mental is the mind. It includes concepts of cognitive, intellectual, thinking, and the physical notion of the human head. People use their minds to think, learn, problem solve, and create. People use their minds to create ideas, concepts, thoughts, habits, and disciplines. It is through our mind we are able to process the holistic teachings through storytelling. The intellectual growth involves learning the history of our families, artistic skills in basket weaving, and carving totem poles. *Nonny* Amanda provided me with a positive learning environment by teaching me our heritage, beliefs, and a wealth of stories.

The emotions are our feelings. This dimension includes components of traditional values of love, affection, understanding, hate, fear, dislike, and misunderstandings. Stories provide emotions; they give us an expression of our feelings and attitudes. Through the emotional component, my grandmother taught me how to love my family and try to understand other people's feelings. She always reinforced the fact that family is the most important part of our life. As a family unit, we have to take care of each other, protect each other and support one another in all aspects of life. We help each other through difficult times and sad times, even when we disagree with one another.

Some of the stories my grandmother told me years ago didn't have meaning until I grew older. Now I reflect back to my grandmother's words and I say, "Yes, now I understand because I have experienced what these values are in order to make it meaningful to my life. I was able to find my own truth in the stories through my experience."

As I take you through my journey, you have to remember that my stories are strips of red and yellow cedar bark. My basket is almost complete. I have woven the red cedar which is the four components called physical, spiritual, emotional, and mental. The weaving is made strong using the yellow cedar to tighten the weaving in my basket. Each strip of red and yellow cedar represents a story. This is my first basket full of stories. As I grow stronger and I become a more knowledgeable Haida woman, I will weave all these components together again. I will weave another basket full of stories. My next basket will be an elegant basket with more intricate and elaborate designs to indicate I have gained more knowledge of my Haida language and culture. I have woven a beautiful basket full of marvellous elaborate stories. I am proud of my basket full of stories.

Raven and Woman Design

Listen to our Elders

Listen to our Elders. They have the wisdom and knowledge of our traditions and culture. They are the true professors to teach us our songs, dances, language, and stories. Our Elders are the link and pathway to regenerating our culture.

Listen to our Elders. They are willing to teach our children how to respect themselves. Our children will learn to respect themselves and they will learn to respect others. Our Elders are eager to teach them how to care and share.

Listen to our Elders. They are willing to teach our children how to preserve the knowledge to make different medicines. Come quickly, our Elders are waiting patiently to teach their children and grandchildren.

Listen to our Elders. They are the library books for our culture. Our history is etched in their minds and hearts to be passed on orally to our people. Our Elders are dying. Every time an Elder dies, we are losing a wealth of knowledge and culture.

Listen to our Elders. They are the roots to the survival of our history and language. Make a positive decision to learn from our Elders. You will be proud of your heritage, culture, and identity as First Nations people.

Education and Culture

Culture is like a tree. When there is a storm, if the roots are strong, the tree will hold. Recent history has weakened our roots. Our people are now getting back our strength. Education is another way to strengthen our roots.
Sargent & Wilson, 1995

Education and culture is an integral part of our lives. They cannot be separated. In this generation we must obtain an appropriate education to survive in this challenging, competitive and technological world. Our children are our most valuable resource. They are the enjoyment of the present generation. They are our hope for the future. They are our future leaders. It is imperative to teach our children their culture. It is essential they get an appropriate education.

All the leaders must encourage their children to learn their languages, traditions, and culture. All First Nations organizations must make rules and regulations to support the children and adults to pursue their goals in education whether their goals is to become a teacher, lawyer, nurse, doctor, carpenter, hairdresser, bookkeeper, or cook. Our people must develop skills, competencies, knowledge, and understanding in this evolving world. We must never lose our identity as First Nations people. Regardless of how young or how old you are, if you have the determination to succeed, you will surely accomplish your goals.

When our children accomplish their goals to become educated, it is vital the leaders utilize and employ the educated First Nations people's knowledge and expertise in their communities, schools, and governments. We must utilize each person in every area of education and experience to regain self-sufficiency and work towards self-government for all our people. When our people can work towards a common goal to obtain an education and regain our languages and culture, we will be a proud powerful Nation. When a Nation loses its culture, the Nation dies.

Trials and Tribulations

Do not judge me by the color of my skin; do not judge me by the clothes I wear. Do not make preconceptions of my character. Do not label me. Do not make assumptions about who I am. Do not hurt me for no valid reasons. Judge me for the person I am; I have a good heart. I have knowledge, history, and stories embedded in my heart, mind, and soul. I have empowered myself to be self-motivated. I have built my self-esteem and through resilient will, fortitude, and determination, I have accomplished my goals to be a writer, weaver, and teacher. I am a strong-spirited, hard-working Haida woman. I am who I am. No one can take that away from me.

Our lives and journeys are riddled with trials and tribulations. Life can be very unfair at times when you make mistakes. You may feel distraught, shattered, and overwhelmed, but making a mistake will not destroy your life. Learning is a lifelong process; we all learn something new everyday.

When you make a mistake in your professional career, your marriage, your relationships, or your daily life, you try to make the best of the situation. Don't beat yourself up and don't punish yourself. Some mistakes may be minor detail, perhaps silly mistakes or dreadful mistakes. You learn from these mistakes to improve your life and you learn to make better choices and decisions.

When mistakes and complications arise in your life, you must find reassurance and comfort in talking to a friend, family member, husband, or colleague. Don't go through these difficult times by yourself. Communication is imperative and essential in your career and daily life. Talk to a genuine friend about your challenges, disappointments, and frustrations, as well as your hopes and dreams. When you get other people's perspective, you find the complications are not as devastating as you may think.

When you make a mistake, the best remedy to overcome any of life's complications is to go for a walk, cry, laugh, or pray. Go for a long walk in the fresh air to clear your mind. Walk in solitude to free yourself from the sorrows and regrets. When you are feeling sad, go ahead and cry. Crying is a healing medicine. Cry and then dry your tears. You are able to gain a more positive attitude. Laughter and humor is good medicine for the soul. Often mistakes may be minor or sometimes the mistake isn't even your fault. You can find humor in life's complications and when you laugh, it is a good healing medicine. Pray and ask for guidance and direction. The power of prayer will make you feel good and lift your spirit. Pray and ask your guardian angels to give you guidance, direction, and support. You will feel more confident and you will be able to strive toward a better tomorrow

When you make a mistake, you will grow wiser and you will not make the same mistake again. You will learn to forgive yourself. When the mistake is not yours, you will learn that the people who are "throwing stones" at you are not worth the stress and tears. When others are making false judgements or defaming your character, you must maintain your integrity and be strong and always keep a positive spirit. Perhaps the saying, "what goes around comes around" will be the reward for the people who throw stones.

You will strive to live everyday to the fullest. When you wake up in the morning, you will leave yesterday behind and you will carve a more positive future. Life is a precious gift and life is a daily challenge. We all live and learn through trails and tribulations.

I Believe

I believe there are misconceptions that all First Nation's education is paid for by the government. There are rules, regulations, policies, and stipulations enforced by each Band. Ironically, not all First Nations people's education is paid for. There are different rules for people who live On-Reserve and Off-Reserve. There are people who are labelled as Status and Non-status Indians. We are called Indians, First Nations, Natives, and Aboriginals. I believe that education is the most important tool we need to survive in this world. I believe that every person regardless of race, creed, or color has the right to an education.

I believe it is important to provide a safe and healthy environment for all students, a place where they can develop their potential. They need a place to acquire skills and contribute in the evolving modern society.

I believe all students need a challenging and supportive environment to learn. They need to learn their roles, rights, and responsibilities in today's society and in the future.

I believe all teachers should be open, supportive, and be knowledgeable to provide high-quality education to all students. All teachers must make every effort to utilize role models, Elders, parents, and leaders within the community. The purpose for involving the community is to eliminate apprehensions and misunderstandings and encourage students to take pride in themselves, their community, and their heritage.

I believe all parents, band councils, and First Nations leaders must make education a top priority for all First Nations children. All representatives must work collaboratively together to provide top quality education for all First Nations students.

I believe it is essential to have mutual respect, communication, and co-operation between all the stakeholders to ensure there is a safe environment and all academic and education tools are presented to all First Nations people.

I believe parents are the first teachers for their children. It is the duty and responsibility of each parent to read to their children to increase their child's reading comprehension, word recognition, and enhance their reading skills.

I believe all parents should talk with their children and provide balance and consistency in their daily lives. They should give them support and encouragement in accomplishing their children's educational goals. When children come from a healthy home, their self-esteem and pride will increase and they will be successful in the education system.

I believe our children must have an education and retain our values, language, and culture. Education is the key to achieving our needs, aspirations, and maintaining our language and culture.

I believe in the saying, "It takes a community to teach a child." The community involves all the parents, teachers, principals, school board members, superintendents, the Aboriginal Education Council, First Nations leaders, Hereditary Chiefs, band councils, and provincial and federal governments. If this community cannot work together, it is the child that suffers.

I believe our children are our most important resources. They are our future leaders, our link to the past generations, and our hope for the future generations. They are our champions. I believe education is the key to our future.

Arthur Collison

Tatzen Collison

Erica Collison

Paul White

Pansy Collison

Amanda Edgars, Isaac Edgars

Mrs. Hunter, Chief Thasi, Mrs. Russ

Amanda Edgars

Protecting our Land

We the Original Peoples of this Land know the Creator put us here. The Creator gave us Laws that govern all our relationships to live in harmony with nature and mankind. The Laws of the Creator defined our rights and responsibilities. The Creator gave us our spiritual beliefs, our languages, our culture, and a place on Mother Earth which provided us with all our needs. We have maintained our freedom, our languages, and our traditions from time immemorial. We continue to exercise the rights and fulfill the responsibilities and obligations given to us by the Creator for the land upon which we were placed. The Creator has given us the right to govern ourselves and the right to self-determination. The rights and responsibilities given to us by the Creator cannot be altered or taken away by any other Nation.
Declaration of the First Nations; Assembly of First Nations Conference, December, 1980

On March 17, 1997, the *Tsath Lan*as Eagle clan members named their Hereditary Chief for their lands located at Naden Harbour. Ken Edgars was named Hereditary Chief. The esteemed women who walked Ken Edgars into the hall were Mrs. June Russ and Mrs. Hunter. These women come from another clan; they were the witnesses and put on his Chieftainship blanket. He was named Chief *Thasi* after one of the *Tsath Lanas* Chiefs from Naden Harbour. Chief *Thasi* has two official spokespersons. His spokespersons are Terry Hamilton and Pansy Collison. They have the duty to assist their Chief in all aspects of economic developments, social responsibilities, political issues, Council of Haida Nations business, and family functions.

Chief *Thasi* is the land chief; therefore, he has the responsibility to maintain, protect, and sustain the lands at Naden Harbour. He is currently starting up a business on these lands. He plans to open a sports lodge and eco-tourism business. His major goal is to employ local people and operate a gift shop where the Haida people have an opportunity to market their arts and crafts at the Kung Lodge Resort. Ken Edgars represents his clan in an honorable fashion and he works hard in a proactive manner to sustain the lands at Naden Harbour.

Our clan has two territories located at Naden Harbour and land on Langara Island. In the early 1800s, Chief *Thasi* passed the lands of Salmon River, Kung, Davidson Creek, and Naden River down to our clan. During those days the Haida people had their own names for the rivers, creeks, and villages. After the arrival of the Europeans, the names were changed. The *Tsath Lanas* people called Kung the most beautiful village on Haida Gwaii.

Nonny Amanda's great grandparents and ancestors helped each other build their houses at Kung. During those days there were about twenty houses built and nearly three hundred people occupied the village. Then the small pox and other diseases decimated many of the Haida people, killing them by the thousands. The surviving Haida people all moved to one village, now called Old Massett.

The village of Kung was deserted in 1884, when all the surviving members of the clan moved to Old Massett Reserve. However, according to oral history, our clan always travelled back and forth to different villages. They stayed at Kung to gather all the rich food resources from their surrounding lands at Naden Harbour. Naden River was the area filled with plenty of ducks, and the surrounding rivers and creeks supplied our clan with salmon and an abundance of cedar bark, berries, sea foods, and spruce roots.

Davidson Creek is the undisputable land that belongs to our clan. This creek is located directly beside Naden River. The tributaries extend to Otard Creek. The original Haida name for Davidson Creek was called Sawbull Creek. This was the original name before the Europeans changed the name to Davidson Creek. *Nonny* Amanda told me our clan chose the best lands at Naden Harbour and Langara Island. During those days the Haida people were honorable people. They respected the Chief of each land, area, and territory. Before they went to gather food on another Chief's land, they asked for permission to enter that land. Their system of land ownership and social systems were intact and greatly appreciated by all the other tribes along the Northwest Coast. The Haida people had their own systems of laws and knowledge of their own matrilineal systems and origins.

Since time immemorial our clan held the fundamental Aboriginal Rights and title to these lands. We have never signed any treaty, nor have we been extinguished by treaty. Our lands have never been bought by the government. No one has the rights to make any kind of economic developments on our lands. The title to our land is woven with our history, politics, stories, and moral obligations. We are the true owners and we will continue to protect our lands. Our Hereditary Chief *Thasi* has inherited the rights and responsibilities to protect our lands and treat our lands with respect and utilize the resources for the benefit of our people.

The following letter is a matter of public record. Open letter to the Haida people was published on April 21, 1997, in the *Queen Charlotte Observer* and *This Week* newspaper.

> My name is Pansy Collison. I am the spokesperson for Mr. Ken Edgars, who has been named Chief for the lands at Naden Harbour. My grandmother held these lands in her name for over eighty years. These lands were passed down to her from her uncles and her great grandfathers. To confirm ownership of these lands, our great grandfathers and great uncles are buried on these lands as a symbolic identification

of where our traditional and territorial lands are on Haida Gwaii.

After my grandmother, the late Amanda Edgars, died on July 30, 1987, we have been making every effort to stop the issuing of forest permits, road developments, silver culture permits, angling guide licenses, fishing lodges or any other developments on our lands. We have been denied our fundamental democratic rights to speak up in protecting our lands from further destruction.

Our lands of Haida Gwaii is being raped and destroyed for far too many years. Every week in the *Observer* there is proposed Forest developments and five year silver culture plans. Now our families have officially named Ken Edgars as Chief for our lands at Naden Harbour, we have taken a position to protect our lands. We will not allow any logging companies to dig up and destroy the graves of our ancestors.

It is time all the Haida people and Hereditary Chiefs spoke up in a united voice to stop all the logging companies from stripping the lands of Haida Gwaii. If anyone has taken a plane to fly over the Islands of Haida Gwaii, you will see most of our Islands are stripped clean. What will we have left for our children, grandchildren and great grandchildren? The resources are being stripped right before our eyes. How many more years are we going to sit back and watch barge loads of our trees shipped off our Islands? Each barge load represents millions and millions of dollars. Years ago, Chief William Matthews said, "Look they're taking away our Islands and nobody cares". Every time a barge load of logs went through Massett Inlet, *Nonny* Amanda said, "The white men are stripping our Islands. Every time I see the barges go by my house, it makes me cry." Perhaps even today our ancestors and our Haida Elders who passed on before us are 'weeping'.

Before European contact, our ancestors lived a magnificent independent and self-reliant life. Their substance and survival depended on the land and sea. Members of each village, clan, and family were the teachers for their children. They taught them how to survive, how to respect the lands and sea. We were taught how to observe, utilize, and respect the lands of Haida Gwaii. Our great grandparents learned through observation and practice. They taught the young people the art of hunting, fishing, trapping, food gathering, and food preparation. They taught their children their identity, who they are, where they come from, what is their clan and crest, who are their families. They taught them the art of building strong shelters, longhouses, and making clothing and tools. They taught them the art of building canoes, longhouses, totem poles, and the great skill of carving in argillite and cedar. They taught their children their language, culture, traditions, beliefs, and customs. We had a powerful generation of great Haida warriors and honorable leaders. We have strong Haida women who were our matriarchs, who were all held in the 'highest esteem'. Our great grandfathers and our ancestors were powerful people.

Today, our generation is different. Times have changed, but the end result is we must work together to protect our Islands from further destruction. On April 26, 1997, our clan will oppose, speak against, and reject any proposed forestry development, road building, or silver culture developments in the vicinity of Davidson Creek, Salmon River or Kung.

If we all work together in a united way, we can stop our Islands from being stripped. We need to stop the issuing of any further forest developments and secure these lands for our children. Many of our

Haida people are unemployed. Every logging company on Haida Gwaii has employed only a 'handful' of Haida men. Many years ago, the logging industry was dominated by the First Nations men. Over these past few years, if you take statistics of how many Haida men are employed on the Islands of Haida Gwaii, you will find less than one dozen men employed at every logging camp. The unemployment rate of our people is grim. We have the opportunity to utilize the resources on Haida Gwaii to employ our people. We can engage in spacing, pruning, planting and all kinds of silver cultural activities and become self-sufficient through the harvesting rights of our own lands. We have the rights to build our own homes on our own lands, reinforce the trapping industry and develop our own resources.

We invite all the Hereditary Chiefs, Haida people and interested people to support us in our efforts to stop the issuing of further forestry permits. A pubic viewing will be held at the Massett Community hall from 10:00 a.m. to 4:00 p.m. on April 26, 1997. We look forward to all the Haida people's support.

Our concerns were addressed as follows:

The proposal has not taken into consideration the historic features and values of the *Tsath Lanas* clan. Our burial grounds and trap lines are located in the vicinity of Kung and South Davidson Creek. We will not allow the logging companies to destroy the burial grounds of our ancestors. We do not go into your graveyards or backyards to dig up and destroy your ancestors' burial grounds. What gives you the right to dig up the graves of our ancestors?

The culturally modified trees are not clearly identified and not clearly shown on the development plan maps. We want to have the culturally modified trees inventory identified and where all the culturally modified trees are found at Davidson

Creek. There is evidence that all the trees were cut. This has not left the culturally modified trees intact and destroys the growth of these trees.

The development plans will destroy the sensitive areas and wildlife habitat areas. Plus the logging practices will and has destroyed the spawning beds for the salmon runs.

The present forest plans by the current logging company does not have substantial compliance with the operational planning regulations and part three of the forest practice code of British Columbia Act. For example: There is a practice of 'Cole decking' taking place all over the Islands of Haida Gwaii. This is a result of the logs breaking off the barges, booming grounds and dumping the logs. There is also logs sinking all over the British Columbia coast and there are logs in all the coves and all around Naden Harbour. When is this going to stop? There are millions of logs that are dumped into the sea and laying a drift on the Islands and along the British Columbia coast. This represents millions and millions of dollars of waste due to the present logging practices. This is common practice and we strongly object to this type of logging practices and recommend the forest practice code of British Columbia Act stop all this waste and address this in their policies.

There are piles of logs laying all over the Islands because there wasn't sufficient amount of logs for a truck load. The logging companies leave these logs to rot. This is an unacceptable logging practice, which must be addressed and appropriate protection measures must be enforced by the forest practice codes act.

There are no proper docks to load the logs on the barges. When you estimate all the logs lying on the beaches all over the Coast, this is enough to supply several pulp mills and local sawmills for approximately twenty years. Ironically, this is covered by insurance. The reality is they are squandering our resources and this must be stopped. Therefore, we are recommending an immediate halt to this type of destruction on our lands.

The proposed forestry development will destroy the Marbled Murrelet nesting habitat. Marbled Murrelets are a threatened species in Canada and they use the forests in Davidson Creek and surrounding areas at Naden Harbour. Marbled Murrelets is dependent on old growth forests and nests in most watersheds, if suitable stands of old growth habitat remain. Marbled Murrelets appear to require mossy platforms in the branches of large conifer trees for nesting. These birds are threatened by logging practices when this type of suitable habitat is lost. We want to have additional research and additional information collected from Davidson Creek on nesting habitat of the Marbled Murrelet. Essentially, this means the proposed forestry development cannot be issued to ensure substantial amounts of old growth forest remains at Davidson creek. Failure to address this is a major deficiency.

There is no evidence that hydrological regimes and the physical features of in stream habitats in the large clear cuts on the north sides of the watersheds have recovered. Clear evidence of this must be produced before any forestry permits are issued.

This proposal will also destroy the old growth habitat for dependent species, wildlife species dependent on specific habitats and there is clearly no identification of important fish and wildlife habitats requiring protection.

On May 8, 1997 the following appeared in the Observer: "Ministry issues permit for Davidson Creek area." My immediate response was total'"blatant disregard' to the concerns of our clan. With permit in hand from the Ministry of Forests, the logging company this week began punching a road into South Davidson Creek at the bottom of Naden Harbour. The District Manager stated the logging company had met every obligation and more in applying for the permit and without any concrete reason for withholding a permit she was compelled to issue it.

I was stunned, surprised, and very disheartened by the approval because there was no discussion, no meeting, nothing to respond to our concerns about the destruction that continues to occur on our territorial lands at Naden Harbour. It's blatant disregard of our requests. I told the district manager she's forced us into a corner here and she responded in the observer for all the public to see and stated, "It's your call now."

It's "our call now." So let's get more specific. These are our specific concerns we addressed:

The Landing sites: There are logs left at the landing sites. We recommend the wood left along the landing sites be broken down for quicker regeneration. The logs on log landings, dry land shorts, dumping grounds, rotten log stumps and high stumps should be broken down with log chippers to help speed up fertilization. Has these methods been taken into consideration? We recommend this be taken into consideration by the Ministry of Forests to implement into the Forest Practice Codes.

Road deactivation: We are concerned about the lack of protection of the salmon. There is no shade for the survival of the salmon. The salmon need natural shade. The creeks are stripped clean and there are no natural surroundings and the salmon cannot survive due to the natural predators. We recommend the Ministry of Forests implement policies to re-shade the tributaries.

We are concerned about the tree length falling. In an average break, there is ten to twenty feet of 'shatter' on broken wood. The companies are wasting good saw logs by shattering the logs. The bigger the logs the more shatter. The reality is this amounts to thousands and thousands of dollars of waste by the logging companies. We recommend policies be reinforced to stop this type of practice.

The investigation and research requests we addressed are as follows:

We want an investigation on the first five years of the logging companies cutting permits. What logs have been left behind at the logging sites? What is left behind in the block areas?

We want an investigation at Stanley Creek. What is under

all those moulds? Why couldn't the tree planters do any tree planting in this area? Why were they hitting solid ground? We want this land uncovered to produce evidence there has been high grading done on our lands.

How much area of 'back hoe trails' is taken up by the logging company? There is obviously second growth, but our major concern is in another ten years these 'back hoe trails' will be grown over. We want a study done to have facts, statistics and research completed and documented. How much area will be taken away due to the back hoe trails?

Rock quarries: We want to know how many hectares of rock quarries there is on the Islands of Haida Gwaii. How many areas do these rock quarries take?

We request a marine study done around the entire area of Naden Harbour and we request studies on the seepage, spills, oil seepage, and contamination done at Naden Harbour.

In regards to the natural forest sometimes a tree falls or rots. The trees feed on the trunks of the tree and die. Does anyone in the Department of Forestry know how long the natural forest will feed on itself? According to my studies, it takes eighty years to fall the trees that have second growth stumps. There is evidence of the old stumps. Does anyone in the Ministry of Forest department know how long it is going to take stumps to break down? If you take into consideration the fact that the stumps take many years to break down, the reality is there is going to be a mass of stumps left in the next 160 years. We recommend that the stumps be cut down so the forest can re-generate faster. We are thinking seriously about the re-generation of the forest in the future. There will be no place to plant trees. This is the reason why we recommend breakage of stumps. This method is implemented in the United States. They are already using the stumps as pulp. The stumps can be cut or chipped down and this can employ our Haida people. Presently the trees are planted ten feet apart. The process has already started to plant between the stumps. Obviously there is less and less to regenerate to grow. We want studies completed on how long it takes stumps to rot down.

Trapping: Our forefathers have trapped on these lands for thousands of years. It is only during these past fifty years that the destruction of the logging has depleted the trapping areas of our people. This is due to all the cutting of the trees that has broken the cycle of the seasons and changed the seasons altogether. Once there is no more logging the natural seasons will return. We request a study done in this regard.

These are the questions we addressed:

- Why are the stumps so high on the Islands of Haida Gwaii compared to the logging areas in the Interior? Will the Ministry of Forests do anything to stop this type of waste?
- What is the required average for 'tops'? In our estimation there is six inches of waste. There is approximately 10 to 20 feet of waste. This can be used as possible pulp. What is the Ministry of Forests doing about this waste?
- We want to know how often does the forest companies monitor or police all the logging companies on Haida Gwaii? Do you do random checks or do you fore-warn each logging company before you do the initial monitoring? We recommend weekly policing checks in isolated areas. Don't say there aren't any funds for this type of monitoring because if the Forest Practices codes took into consideration our recommendations to stop the wastage, these funds could be utilized to do weekly monitoring at the logging companies on Haida Gwaii. (See Forest Practice Code for more policy details) We recommend the Ministry of Forests hire experienced Haida loggers to monitor these areas.
- There is no evidence that hydrological regimes and the physical features of in-stream habitats in the large clear cuts on the north sides of the watersheds have

recovered. Clear evidence of this must be produced before any forestry permits are issued. We want this matter addressed.

- How many hectares of rock queries take up space on the Islands?
- Why is there so much waste for the average 'tops'?
- Regarding the tree length falling an average break is 10 to 20 feet of 'shatter' on broken wood. Why does this practice continue?
- How many hectares are there planted per year at Davidson Creek?
- How many hectares are logged, spaced and pruned each year?
- How long before a logged off area is spaced?

We specifically request the following clean up be done on our lands of Davidson Creek, and our surrounding lands at Naden Harbour.

Major clean up on rock pits and rock quarries.

There is no cement protection along the sea and waters of Naden Harbour. Throughout all these years, there is mud running steadily into the sea affecting the sea life and therefore causes grease and oil which is destroying the sea life and sea foods which we depend on. Why isn't there a cement area built to protect the sea life and sea foods? Has there ever been a marine study done on how the logging affects the sea and sea life? How much mud has literally destroyed the natural sea life? How much bark is in the waters of Naden Harbour affecting the sea life? We request these concerns be addressed by Ministry of Forests and an adequate study regarding our concerns; plus we request that the logging companies build an appropriate cement protection to prevent further destruction of the sea life in Naden Harbour.

There is billions of dollars for forest renewal which we recommend to be used to clean up these areas. There is enough logs lying around and enough work to employ Haida men for over a year to patch up the rock quarries and clean up the rock pits for future growth in these areas. We recommend these dollars be accessed to employ our Haida men.

It is my understanding that when there is an economic downswing in the forest industry, especially in isolated areas, the logging companies have been allowed to "high grade." If companies are permitted to squander forest resources, the logging quotas should be cut immediately. We recommend the quotas be cut.

As the spokesperson for our Hereditary Chief, Mr. Ken Edgars we continue to work together to protect our lands. We stand firm in protecting our lands at Naden Harbour. Since time immemorial our clan has owned these lands. Our great *Tsath Lanas* ancestors have used and conserved the resources of these lands with great care and respect. They governed the lands, waters, salmon, and the animals. This is written in our songs, stories, and totem poles. Our history is written in the hearts of the Haida Elders and our history is present in our language at the potlatches and our history is present in our spiritual beliefs.

Our sovereignty is our Haida culture. Our Aboriginal rights and title to these lands have never been extinguished by treaty or by any agreement with the Crown. We did not sell this land and we did not agree to have our lands destroyed by the logging companies or any other economic developments.

Our people have suffered many injustices, but today we stand proud to protect our lands from further injustice. In the past, the Ministry of Forests or logging companies have not consulted with our clan about any forest or other economic developments on our territorial lands. These developments have not included our hopes, aspirations, needs, and participation in protecting our resources.

Our clan will continue to exercise our sovereignty and our fundamental Aboriginal rights in protecting our lands. It is our right and duty to protect our lands for the future of our grandchildren.

Eagle Design

What does Culture Mean To Me?

Culture is the foundation from which we experience life, apply meaning and develop our world view. How we learn, how we think, and our life experiences are determined by our culture. Culture is the day to day living of one's life. It is a safe place of human bonding.
Wilson & Napolean, 1994

Culture is my traditions, beliefs, values, and identity. Every culture has their own values, beliefs, and identity. I come from the *Tsath Lanas* Eagle clan and I come from the lands of Haida Gwaii.

Culture is the language I speak and how I understand my native language. I am a functional Haida speaker and my language is essential and the most typical expression of our culture.

Culture is where I come from and how my family passes on our stories and history. Stories are part of our oral culture. Our history is written and carved on our totem poles, regalia, and crests. I display my crests on my vests and all the carved jewellery that I wear daily.

Culture is the songs I sing and how I perform each dance. We perform at all the feasts and potlatches. Our songs and dances are integral to our culture. We cannot separate our songs from our culture and history.

Culture is how I dress. I wear my crests on all my clothing, vests, button blankets, and blazers. I sew all my own designs on my blazers and clothing. When I wear my crests on my clothing, this identifies who I am and where I come from.

Culture is my surroundings of where I live. It doesn't matter where I live; I am able to make a statement in who I am. Culture is my knowledge of our traditions and stories. Culture is how I present myself in my immediate surroundings.

Culture is how I think and feel, and it teaches me how to love my family. I was taught our traditional values of compassion, humility, courage, consideration, sensitivity, gentleness, and how to be helpful. My life experience's has taught me how to think and feel towards other people.

Culture is how I express myself through my skills, talents, and artistic abilities. I am a weaver, artist, and storyteller. I make button blankets, dream catchers, vests, traditional regalia, and drums. I am a leader and positive role model in the art of Haida songs and dances.

Culture is the way I provide my family with food, water, shelter, clothing, and transportation. Culture is the food I eat from the land and sea that keeps me strong and healthy. Culture is how much I love to eat Indian food – razor clams, smoked sockeye, *oolicans*, seaweed, deer meat, grease, and fried bread.

Culture is how I pass on my knowledge to my children and how I am able to teach the Northwest Coast traditional culture in the classroom. Culture is how I am able to share my knowledge to keep our traditions intact for our future generations of grandchildren.

Culture is continuously evolving and changing. Each generation of culture is different. Our great ancestor's days were different from our culture of today. My generation is different and changing compared to my children's generation. The art is changing and the expressions of the young people are changing through the modern day language and lifestyles.

Culture is an evolving process. It is up to each individual to capture their traditional culture and maintain their language and identity. Each person has a culture. It is evidenced by how they live their life.

My culture is how I eat, how I think, how I dress, how I live, how I talk, how I sing, how I dance, how I love, how I care, and how I share my traditions, beliefs, and stories with others. This is my culture. This is how I keep the Haida culture alive.

My Loved Ones

I love my children. They light up my life.
I love to see their beautiful faces.
I love to see their happy smiles.
I love to hear my children laugh.
  I believe my children will accomplish their goals.
  I believe my children will make good choices in their lives.
  I believe they will be successful in their education.
  I believe my children will be positive role models.
    I love my son. I love my daughter. They make me happy.
    I love to give my children hugs and kisses.
    I love to see my children grow and mature every day.
    I love to hear my children say, "I love you Mom".
      I will always be there to guide and protect my children.
      I will always be there when they are sad, lonely or in pain.
      I will always worry about my children as long as I live.
      I will be happy when I know my children are safe and healthy.

I see you, I hear you,
My heart knows,
My spirit knows,
I will always be there for you,
I will always love my children

(top left to right) Paul White Jr., Gertie White, Paul White Sr., Isaac White; (bottom left to right) Johnny White, Pansy Collison

Stolly White

(left to right), Ben White, John Paul White, Tatzen Collison, Pansy Collison, Stolly Collison

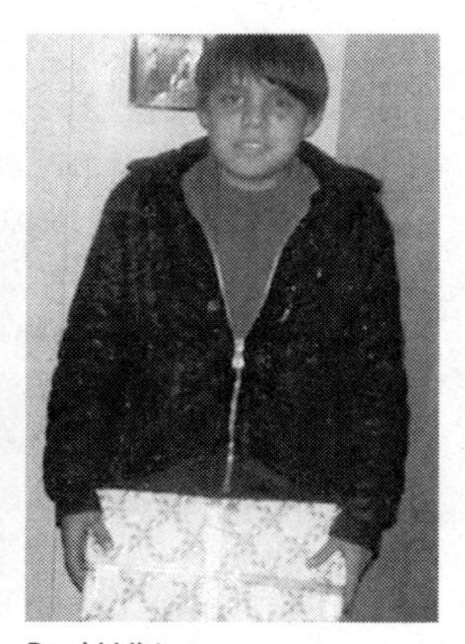

Paul White

Isaac White, Jayson White

Herman White, Johnny White

Gertie White, Paul White

(left to right) Art Collison, Stolly Collison, Pansy Collison

Dean Edgars

Haida Glossary

Cheegan – male going to the bathroom
Chinny – grandfather
Clun – stop
Gaa-daa – dear one
Gisg'wayah – North Island or Langara Island
Gitingow – devil's club
Gowkith – take food home
How-a – thank you
How-wheet – come here
Hucksta – let's go
Kiid K'iyaas – old tree
Kuni – aunty
Muck-tul-lay – Victoria (The City of)
Nonny – grandmother
Sa'donna – merit eggs
Sic Dim Dolla – referring to a dollar
Skajuu – bald head
Skou-un – salmon berries
Yanne-goowah – big animal

References

Adams, D., & Murkowski, J. (1988). *The Queen Charlotte Islands reading series.* Vancouver, BC: Pacific Educational Press, University of British Columbia.

Armstrong, J. (1987). Traditional Indigenous education: A natural process. *Canadian Journal of Native Education,* 14 (3), 14.

Asch, Michael. (1988) *Home and native land: Aboriginal rights and the Canadian Constitution.* Toronto: Nelson Canada.

Battiste, M., & Barman, J. (1995). *The circle unfolds: First Nations education in Canada.* Vancouver, BC: UBC Press.

Beck, M. (1989). *Heroes & heroines: Tlingit-Haida legend.* Anchorage, AK: Alaska Northwest Books.

Bell, R. (1993). Journeys. In L. Jaine (Ed.), *Residential schools: The stolen years* (pp. 8-16). Saskatoon, SK: University Extension Press, University of Saskatchewan.

Beynon, J. (2008). *First Nations teachers: Identity and community, struggle and change.* Calgary, AB: Detselig Enterprises Ltd.

Blackman, M. B. (1982). *During my time: Florence Edenshaw Davison, a Haida woman.* Vancouver, BC: Douglas & McIntryre.

Boelscher, M. (1989). *The curtain within: Haida social and mythical discourse.* Vancouver, BC: UBC Press.

British Columbia Forest Practices Code: Standards with Revised Rules and Field Guide References, FS 2451.

Cajete, G. (2000). Indigenous knowledge: The Pueblo metaphor of Indigenous education. In M. Battiste (Ed.), *Reclaiming Indigenous voice and vision* (pp. 181-191). Vancouver: UBC Press.

Canada. Canadian Intergovernmental Conference Secretariat. (1983). *Federal-Provincial Conference of First Ministers on Aboriginal Constitutional Matters.* (E 92 A53 1983 A15). Ottawa, ON: Author.

Collison, A. (1993). Healing myself through our Haida traditional customs. In L. Jaine (Ed.), *Residential schools: The stolen years.* (pp. 35-42). Saskatoon, SK: University Extension Press, University of Saskatchewan.

Cogo N., & Cogo R. (1983). *Haida History*, Ketchikan, Alaska: Ketchikan Indian Corporation.

Cooley, R. E., & Ballenger, R. (1982). Culture retention programs and their impact on Native American cultures. In R. N. St. Clair & W. L. Leap (Eds.), *Language renewal among American Indian tribes: Issues, problems, and prospects.* Arlington, VA: National Clearing House for Bilingual Education.

Cruikshank, J. (1995). *Life lived like a story* (3rd ed.). Vancouver, BC: University of British Columbia Press

Curtis, E. S. (1970). *The North American Indian* (vol. 11). New York: Johnson Reprint Co.

Damm-Akiwenzie, K., & Armstong, J. (Eds.). (1996). *Gatherings.* Volume VII, Penticton, BC: Theytus Books Ltd.

Davies, B., & Harre, R. (1999). *Positioning: The discursive production of selves.* Retrieved November 3, 2007, from *www.masey.ac.nz/~Alock/position.htm*

Drew, L. (1982) *Haida: Their Art and Culture.* Surrey, British Columbia, Canada: Hancock House Publishers Ltd.

Enrico, J. (1986). Word order, focus, and topic in Haida. *International Journal of American Linquistics,* 52 (2), 91-123.

Enrico, J. (1994). The Haida Dictionary. *Haida Laas 1*(8), 1, 3, 6.

Enrico, J. (Ed.). (1995). *Skidegate Haida myths and stories.* Skidegate, BC: Queen Charlotte Islands Press

Enrico, J, & Stuart, W. B. (1996). *Northern Haida Songs.* Lincoln and London: University Nebraska Press.

Friesen, V., Archiebald, J., & Jack, R. (1992). *Creating cultural awareness about First Nations: Guide.* Vancouver, BC: Native Indian Teachers Education Program, University of British Columbia.

Gosnell, J. (1996, February 17). This Adawak took a century to compose. *The Weekend Sun,* p. A23.

Henley, T. (1989). *Rediscovery: Ancient pathways, new directions.* Vancouver, BC: Western Canada Wilderness Committee.

Holland, D., Lachicotte, W., Skinner, D., & Cain, C. (1998). *Identity and agency in cultural worlds.* Cambridge, MA: Harvard University Press.

Indian Act, R.S., (1984) c.1-5 amended by R.S., 1985, c. 32 (1st Supp.) R.S., 1985, c.27 (2nd Supp.) R.S., 1985, c. 17, 43, 48 (4th Supp.). Sept. 1989, Minister of Supply and Services Canada, 1989.

Jensen, D. & Brooks. C. (1991). *In celebration of our survival: The First Nations of British Columbia.* Vancouver, BC: UBC Press.

Johnson, M. (1987). Canada's Queen Charlotte Islands: Homeland of the Haida. *National Geographic, 172* (1), 102-127.

Kirkness, V. J. (1992). *First Nations and schools: Triumphs and struggles.* Toronto: Canadian Education Association.

MacDonald, G. F. (1994). *Haida monumental art.* Vancouver, BC: UBC Press.

Mercredi, O., & Turpell, M. E. (1993). *In the rapids.* Toronto: Penguin.

Mussell, W., Nicholls, W., & Adler, T. (1991) *Making meaning of mental health challenges in First Nations: A Freirean perspective.* Chilliwack, BC: Sal'I'Shan Institute Society.

National Indian Brotherhood. (1972) *Indian control of Indian education.* A policy paper presented to the Minister of Indian Affairs and Northern Development. Ottawa, ON: National Indian Brotherhood.

Sargent, D., & Wilson E. (1995) *Stepping stones to improved relationships: Aboriginal equity and Northwest Community College.* Terrace, BC: Northwest Community College.

Slapin, B., & Seale, D. (1992). *Through Indian eyes: The Native experience in books for children* (3rd ed.). Philadelphia, PA: New Society Publishers.

Stairs, A. (1993). Learning processes and teaching roles in Native education: Cultural base and cultural brokerage. In S.

Morris, K. McLeod, M. Danesi (Eds.), *Aboriginal languages and education: The Canadian experience* (p. 85-101). Oakville, ON: Mosaic Press.

Sterling, S. (2002). Yetko and Sophie: Nlakapamux cultural professors. *Canadian Journal of Native Education,* 26 (1), 4-10.

Swanton, J. R. (1905a) *Contributions to the ethonology of the Haida.* New York: Leiden, E. J. Brill.

Swanton, J. R. (1905b). *Haida texts and myths, Skidegate dialect.* BAT-B, 29.

Swanton, J. R. (1911). *Haida texts: Masset dialect. AMNH-M 10,* 273-803.

Swanton, J. R. (1912) *Haida. HAIL I. BAE-B* 40, 205-82.

Turner, N. (2004). *Plants of Haida Gwaii.* Winlaw, BC: Sono Nis Press.

Tafoya, T. (1989). Coyote's eyes: Native cognition styles. *Journal of American Indian Education,* Special edition, 1-14.

White, Frederick. (2008). *Ancestral language acquisition among Native Americans: A study of a Haida language class.* Lewiston, NY: The Edwin Mellen Press, Ltd.

Wilson, E., & Napolean, V. (1994). *Enhancing relationships between schools and First Nations families.* Victoria, BC: Ministry of Education

Vaillant, John. (2005). *The Golden Spruce,* Toronto: Alfred A. Knopf.

Index